CREATIVE COUNTERTRADE

Ballinger Series in

BUSINESS IN A GLOBAL ENVIRONMENT

S. Prakash Sethi, Series Editor

Center for Management
Baruch College
The City University of New York

CREATIVE COUNTERTRADE
A Guide to Doing Business Worldwide

KENTON W. ELDERKIN
WARREN E. NORQUIST

BALLINGER PUBLISHING COMPANY
Cambridge, Massachusetts
A Subsidiary of Harper & Row, Publishers, Inc.

International Standard Book Number: 0-88730-183-5

Library of Congress Catalog Card Number: 86-22185

Printed in the United States of America

Library of Congress Cataloging-in-Publication Data

Elderkin, Kenton W.
  Creative countertrade.

  Includes index.
  1. Countertrade. 2. Developing countries—Commerce.
3. Export trading companies. I. Norquist, Warren E.
II. Title.
HF1412.E536 1986   658.8'48   86-22185
ISBN 0-88730-183-5

CONTENTS

LIST OF FIGURES

LIST OF TABLES

PREFACE

The world of international trade is more complicated than ever before. As national economies become increasingly linked to the world economy, the situation will become even more complex. Countertrade, that is, any sale in which payment is not entirely in cash, has become an important element of world trade, especially during the last five years. As a form of international trade, countertrade is growing rapidly. Increasingly, exporting companies either countertrade or they don't sell their products.

Chances are, you are going to run across countertrade sometime in your career if you haven't done so already. Once the exclusive domain of the Soviet Union and Eastern Europe, countertrade today is used around the world in both industrialized and third world countries. A recent federal government survey revealed that sixty-one countries have required countertrade from U.S. exporting companies wishing to sell products in their country. In fact, only about 30 countries out of 171 in the world do not countertrade, and most of these are tiny islands or city states tied to the economies of larger nations that do engage in countertrade. Familiarizing yourself with countertrade, now, will prevent you from being caught off guard when its prospects are suddenly thrust upon your organization.

Thus far, countertrade has been limited chiefly to certain industries: aerospace, chemicals, commodities, and so forth. But as countertrade continues to grow, the list of industries affected will expand. If yours has not been hit already, it may be next.

As a businessperson intent on remaining competitive, you need to read this book. *Creative Countertrade* provides an efficient and effective explanation of countertrade. With this book, you can absorb essential information easily and quickly, and without having to wade through painful academic verbosity. Moreover, *Creative Countertrade* does more than trace the past to the present; it also analyzes and projects future developments in international trade. Thus *Creative Countertrade* sheds light on new angles that offer you a wider range of alternatives and control than that available to most experienced traders.

Frequent references are made throughout *Creative Countertrade* to the role of MNCs (multinational corporations), the Third World, LDCs (less developed countries) and NICs (newly industrialized countries). In this book, *MNC* is used loosely to refer to any business or entity in the developed world engaged in international sales. The term *Third World* is also used loosely and, unless more specifically defined, refers to poorer, less-developed countries. *LDC* and Third World are used interchangeably. *NICs* include such third world countries as India, South Korea, Hong Kong, Taiwan, Singapore, Mexico, Brazil, Israel, and South Africa, which have experienced rapid economic growth rates and an expanded manufacturing export sector.

Creative Countertrade, begins by defining the basic elements of countertrade, such as barter, switch, buyback, and, compensation. It traces the history of countertrade since the Second World War and explains why it has spread across the world. Other topics discussed in the opening chapters include MNCs trying to sell their goods into countries; the mechanics of a representative countertrade contract; the respective roles played by banks, lawyers, and traders in the countertrade transaction; and available sources of information.

The second half of the book examines a new concept called creative countertrade, which includes long-term deals that enable a company to create or expand a series of small businesses. These small businesses export from the host country, and, in so doing, generate such levels of profit and foreign exchange that the company is able to get its own goods inside the host country unopposed. Creative countertrade focuses on small businesses that can be easily replicated and then developed into market niches on the outside.

An area that will be of interest to corporations and fund raisers alike is the use of blocked funds, discussed in detail in the second half of the book. Several suggestions are proposed, among them using these funds to send American students and scientists—or others from the industrial world—to live, work, and learn in third world countries. The benefits are many: the blocked funds are used constructively; the host country earns foreign exchange and pays off its debt; and young men and women gain firsthand experience of third world countries and return home with expertise to offer government, nonprofit institutions, and business.

Other topics related to creative countertrade are examined, such as joint ventures, exporting businesses, and a variety of low-tech and service businesses ideally suited to third world countries.

Finally, the constraints of countertrade are discussed. These include MNC and third world reservations concerning countertrade, the difficulties of doing business in the Third World, and the negative effects of countertrade—hurt cash sales, increased import prices, the creation of a vicious credit circle, increased protectionism, and a reduction of world trade.

The following pages are fully illustrated to give you a fast, clear understanding of countertrade. We believe that no other book on the subject includes such extensive illustration and explanation. Readers new to the subject will definitely wish to begin with Chapter 1. Those familiar with it may wish to skim the first three chapters and begin reading at Chapter 4. We hope that both groups will find their time well spent.

The authors are committed to the principle that the best solution to world trade imbalances is greater integration and cooperation among business people around the globe. They wish to thank Audley Shaw, Director, North American Operations, Jamaica National Investment Promotion Limited, in New York City for his enthusiasm and inspiration during the inception stage of this book.

The authors are indebted to diligent efforts of Barbara Roth of Ballinger, and Sheila Tully, whose superb editing greatly enhanced the readability of this work.

1 TRADITIONAL COUNTERTRADE

The general business community knows little about countertrade. For some the name has a mysterious ring to it, conjuring scenes from *Casablanca* or *Chinatown* of clandestine meetings held in smoke-filled holds at dilapidated piers on foggy nights, away from the prying eyes of government agents and provocateurs.

Asking the *experts* for an explanation often proves unenlightening. Part of the problem is that explanations vary depending on whom one talks to. Jim Walsh, Senior International Economist at the U.S. Department of Commerce, jests, "We know more about Bigfoot than we know about countertrade."[1] A senior manager in a U.K. trading firm quips that countertrade is "a sort of illness."[2] Some people charge that mandated countertrade is protectionism at its most virulent.[3] Others liken countertrade to gambling winnings: A lot of people do it, but not everyone reports it. Is countertrade, then, something only of interest to a James Bond? Is it, as countertrade consultant Roger Davis likes to ask, legal, moral, and nonfattening?[4] Can it be defined more precisely?

Attempts are being made to standardize the many definitions of countertrade and related concepts. Most would agree, however, that countertrade is an umbrella term referring to any transaction where payment is made, at least partially with goods instead of money. In all its forms, countertrade links two transactions—normally indepen-

1

dent under a free trade system—into one agreement. These transactions are the sale of a product by the MNC (multinational corporation) into a country, and the sale of goods out of that country.[5]

THE FORMS OF COUNTERTRADE

Countertrade agreements assume five basic forms, depending on the specifics of four variables: the nature of the goods traded, the percent of payment made in goods, the length of time required for full payment to be made, and the number of parties involved.

The five forms of countertrade are:

1. Barter
2. Buyback
3. Compensation
4. Counterpurchase
5. Switch

Barter (Figure 1-1) is the one-for-one exchange of goods under a single contract with no money involved. It is the simplest form of countertrade because it is an even swap.

Most barter deals are mundane, as in the case of China agreeing to send hogs to Japan in exchange for dairy cows. But some are unusual and innovative. A Swedish rock and roll group, for example, agreed

Figure 1-1.

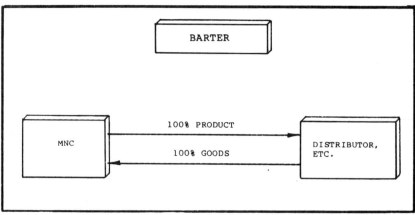

to take coal as payment for its tour in Poland. CBS secured thirty-two one-minute spots of advertising space on Chinese television by agreeing to provide sixty-four hours of programming. CBS, in turn, is selling the space to companies interested in expanding their markets in China, like Boeing and IBM.[6]

Buyback (Figure 1-2) is the delivery of the means to produce goods or services in exchange for manufactured products to be repaid at a later date. Normally a buyback arrangement has some kind of turnkey plant or equipment associated with it.

Certain countries and geographical areas, like China and Eastern Europe, make substantial use of buybacks in their countertrade arrangements. China tends to make small buyback arrangements, while Eastern European countries engage in larger deals. For example, the Sansui Down Factory of the Guizhou Province of China sold high-quality down to a Hong Kong firm in exchange for equipment to upgrade its existing factory.[7] The controversial natural gas deal between Western Europe and the USSR is a buyback transaction. Similarly, the Austrian engineering and steel company, Voest-Alpine, made an agreement to install a steel plant in Italy in exchange for some of the output.[8]

Most buyback deals are self-liquidating, that is, after a certain portion of the product is delivered, the entire plant or equipment becomes the property of the host country. Buyback agreements at the end of the 1970s often took about ten years to complete. Today, because traders have more experience with and confidence in

Figure 1-2.

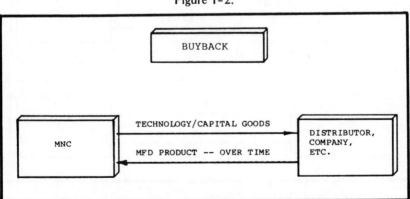

countertrade, deals often extend for as long as fifteen years. At their best buyback arrangements offer long-lasting stable markets, facilitate Western technology transfer, and increase third world production standards. Because of this, countries that mandate countertrade prefer buyback deals to traditional countertrade.

Compensation (Figure 1-3) refers to the ratio (or percent) of the value of the goods countertraded to the value of the product being sold. As the figure shows, cash can move either way, depending on the amount of the compensation.

In one sense, compensation is a term that applies to all countertrade transactions. But compensation is also known as offset. Traditionally, offsets have been associated with defense procurements and large civilian construction projects. An example of how large offsets can be is General Dynamics' 1983 sale of $10 billion worth of F-16s to Turkey. The offset for that transaction was $10.5 billion.[9]

Offsets are either direct or indirect. A *direct offset* occurs when there are close managerial and technological ties between the sale into the host country and the purchase coming out of the country.

Figure 1-3.

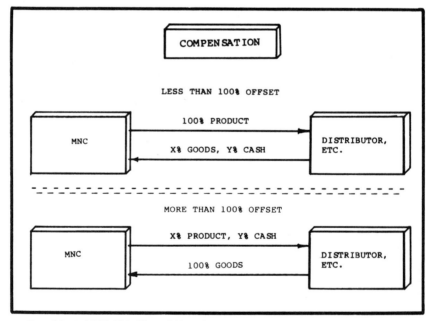

Coproduction agreements are a form of direct offset that require the host country to contribute toward the manufacture of the product being sold there. *Indirect offsets* concern the purchase or exchange of a product or commodity unrelated to the sale of the product in the host country. Such was the case when Boeing sold Saudi Arabia ten 747s worth $1 billion in exchange for 34 million barrels of oil.[10]

Host countries prefer direct offsets because such an arrangement allows them to gain the technical expertise necessary to take care of and maintain equipment themselves and avoid costly long-term maintenance contracts. Direct offsets thus allow nations to maintain political independence in regard to the maintenance of their military equipment. Iran, for example, found itself tied to the United States because it had neither the qualified mechanics nor parts necessary to fly its American built aircraft. Colonel Kadafy in Libya is similarly tied to the Soviet Union today.[11]

Counterpurchase (Figure 1–4) is an exchange of unrelated goods often associated with a third party inside the host country. In this case, the MNC purchases goods from someone else in the country who is paid by the buyer (distributor) in local currency. The counterpurchase transaction can be either the equivalent of two transactions (top of Figure 1–4) or one triangular transaction (bottom of Figure 1–4).

In 1982 Chrysler sent vehicles to Jamaica in exchange for bauxite.[12] General Electric sent Sweden jet engines for Swedish industrial goods.[13] Coke has traded its syrup for the output of a cheese plant it built in the Soviet Union, oranges from orchards it planted in Egypt, tomato paste from a plant it installed in Turkey, beer from Poland, and soft drink bottles from Hungary.[14] In all these examples, the entity purchasing the American products was different from that selling the countertraded goods.

Occasionally, counterpurchase is confused with offset. The primary difference between an offset and a counterpurchase is that an offset is a large takeback often consisting of a variety of goods chosen and received over a period of years; whereas, counterpurchase usually implies a smaller deal comprising a fewer number of items taken back over a shorter period or even on a spot basis.[15] Counterpurchase differs from barter in that it has a cash element whereas barter has none. That is, with counterpurchase, more cash always flows in one direction than the other, usually toward the MNC.

Figure 1-4.

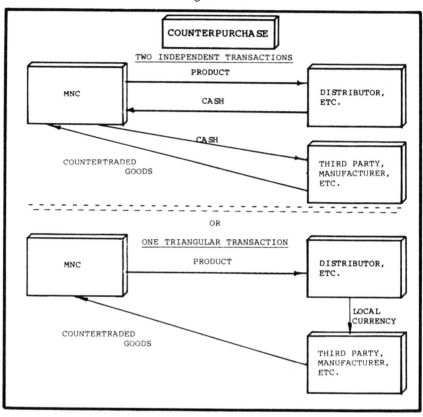

Ninety percent of U.S. nonmilitary countertrade has been counterpurchase. About 5 percent consisted of buybacks, and under 2 percent were barter transactions. In the five years between 1980 and 1984 some $1.8 billion came into the United States through countertrade, almost half of which was purchased for internal use in the company doing the deal.[16]

A *switch* transaction (Figure 1-5) uses at least one third party outside the host country to complete the countertrade leg. Either the MNC's products or the countertraded products are sent through a third country for purchase or distribution. The countertraded goods are then shipped to another country that pays in hard currency.

Switch transactions are advantageous because they enlarge the area from which goods can be taken. ContiTrade, for example, recently

Figure 1-5.

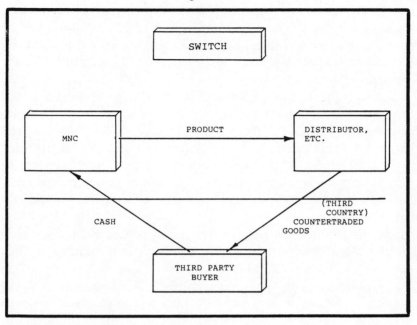

wanted to export corn to Brazil but could not find a bank to finance
the credit risk, in part, because too little was available in Brazil to
take out at the time. East Germany, however, did have products that
could be taken and sold. Barry Westfall, an experienced trader at
ContiTrade, knew that East Germany had a bilateral trade deficit
with Brazil. Thus, he was able to ship the corn to Brazil and have
cruzeiros sent as payment to the Brazilian central bank, which in
turn credited the East German clearing account. East Germany then
shipped the goods to ContiTrade, which sold them for hard currency. Conti was the only private company to participate in this deal,
which took almost a year to execute.[17]

Countertrade deals are increasingly becoming triangular because
triangular arrangements facilitate the movement of goods. Additionally, with the use of computers it has become easier to sort the best
possibilities among large numbers of participants. Countertrade
arrangements are not confined to large conglomerates. Kwik-Way,
of Marion, Iowa, shipped $150,000 worth of machinery to Spain and
took olive oil in return, which it then sold in Lebanon. In a triangular

deal, the same company shipped $150,000 worth of machinery to the USSR, which sent machine tools to Canada, which in turn shipped equipment to be used in Kwik-Way's Marion plant.[18] One of the problems with a switch, however, is that each time goods and services change hands they have to be discounted on each leg of the transaction.[19]

Countertrade is criticized for allowing foreign countries to sell their goods in the United States at the expense of domestic manufacturers. However, for every countertraded dollar exported, less than thirty cents comes back to the United States in countertraded goods. This is because the remaining seventy cents have been sent to other developed countries primarily because of switch transactions. Therefore, the United States gains more from this in income and jobs than it loses.

A switch transaction can also operate in reverse when, for example, the MNC countertrades more products into country A than country A's markets can absorb, country A can then re-export the MNC products in a straight, soft currency cash transaction. With the cooperation of respective governments, the MNC could send its goods into country A, which owes a number of other countries, for "reshipment" to countries willing to accept the MNC's products as repayment of loans. The intent is to use one country as a base to penetrate the protectionism of the regional trading block of which it is a member. Usually, the trading block requires that considerable value be added to the product, which makes this type of transaction difficult.

There are other facets to countertrade in addition to the five forms explained above. Dr. C.G. Alexandrides, director of International Market Information System (IMIS) and professor of management at the University of Georgia, makes the distinction between reactive and proactive countertrade. *Reactive countertrade* occurs when a company initially tries to make the sale in the host country for cash, but when it discovers it has no other choice, tries to find ways of doing countertrade. This type of decisionmaking is often expensive and nonproductive. In such an arrangement between Control Data and the Soviet Union, Control Data agreed to exchange computers for Christmas cards, only to discover later that there wasn't much of a market in the United States for religious cards with "Made in USSR" printed on the back.[20]

Proactive countertrade occurs when a company prepares its countertrade strategy in advance. An example is McDonnell–Douglas's current negotiations with China about setting up joint ventures in which China would make small commercial aircraft for its own domestic airlines, with McDonnell–Douglas supplying the parts. In a similar small countertrade deal, Rank Xerox traded a $100,000 copier to Albania for men's leisure clothes, which Rank Xerox sold to France.[21] Because both McDonnell and Xerox knew they would have to countertrade, they planned the takeback part of the transaction in advance, rather than waiting until they were asked.

The Secretariat of the Organization for Economic Cooperation and Development categorizes countertrade agreements into two types: commercial and industrial. *Commercial compensation* refers to one-shot deals, which normally are relatively small in comparison with industrial compensation. Normally, the transactions are finished within three years. Barter transactions, counterpurchases, and even pre-compensation arrangements (countertraded goods taken in advance and entered on evidence accounts) are considered forms of commercial compensation.

Industrial compensation consists of larger deals involving the sale of industrial equipment, turnkey plants, military hardware, and huge construction projects. Buyback and offset agreements are examples of industrial compensation.

Commercial compensation is the most frequently used form of countertrade. But industrial compensation deals, although fewer in number, comprise a substantial part of the dollar value of current countertrade arrangements.[22]

Chuck Martin, Director of Trade and Countertrade at the Westinghouse Corporation, classifies countertrade deals according to the way the MNC acts: direct and indirect. *Direct countertrade* occurs when the control is in-house (co-production, transfer of technology, investments, and joint ventures) and *indirect countertrade* occurs when a company's purchases are done by a bank or a trading firm. Direct countertrade usually elicits a higher amount of government interest and cooperation. It also allows for more countertrade credits. Indirect countertrade has advantages with respect to financing because it focuses on gaining hard currency.[23]

Reciprocity is an informal countertrade agreement without contractual linkage. It is based on unwritten understandings and carries more weight in third world and socialist countries than in the developed world. Governments in third world countries take a far more active role in their business dealings than do governments in the developed world. When the host government is either party or privy to the activity of the MNC, reciprocity enhances the working relationship between countertrade parties.

The AMF Corporation's dealings with the People's Republic of China illustrates how reciprocity can work. AMF first tried to position itself there as a purchaser in an effort to create goodwill with the Chinese government. Often, selling alone fails to provide real insight into how the markets in a particular country work. One has to buy in order to see the whole picture. This is especially true in China. If outsiders come in as a buyers first, they get a much better reception and more willing help. Thus, a buying mission can often furnish much better marketing information and cooperation than a sales mission.[24]

A *bilateral clearing account* occurs when two nations agree to exchange goods and services over a period of time (usually a year). No foreign exchange is transferred. The transactions are recorded on the books of the two central banks of each of the respective countries, with some currency such as clearing dollars used as a medium of valuation for the goods exchanged. If the accounts swing out of balance by a negotiated amount (20 to 30 percent), the trading or creditor nation stops exporting until the debtor nation exports enough to bring the accounts within the agreed upon differential. The nation in arrears receives an effective interest fee loan based on the average amount it owes during the period. At the period's end, the accounts are cleared either in hard currency or in some form of payment in goods.[25] As far as individual companies are concerned, a bilateral trade agreement acts like a cash transaction. The only countertrade involved concerns the adjustment mechanism used to balance the accounts. The rest of the arrangement is in effect reciprocal open credit between the two countries.

THE NEED FOR COUNTERTRADE

The need for countertrade is proportional to the respective commercial strengths of the buyer and the seller (Figure 1-6). In other words:

Figure 1-6.

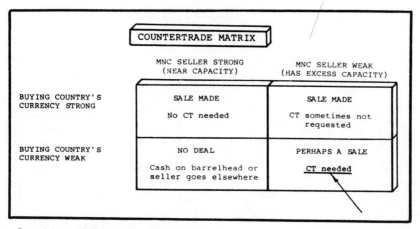

COUNTERTRADE MATRIX

	MNC SELLER STRONG (NEAR CAPACITY)	MNC SELLER WEAK (HAS EXCESS CAPACITY)
BUYING COUNTRY'S CURRENCY STRONG	SALE MADE No CT needed	SALE MADE CT sometimes not requested
BUYING COUNTRY'S CURRENCY WEAK	NO DEAL Cash on barrelhead or seller goes elsewhere	PERHAPS A SALE CT needed

- Countries with balance of payments problems rely more heavily on countertrade than those that do not have those problems.

- Companies whose products do not create strong demand rely more heavily on countertrade.

High-priority items are strategic, have status, or involve the military. Figure 1-7 shows how a host country's import priority levels affect its level of countertrade. Some countries actually have detailed lists assigning priorities to all imported products. Colombia, for example, updates its list routinely. MNCs operating in that country have to be on their toes, making sure they have the latest list so that their requests comply with the law.[26]

High-priority imports are most readily traded for cash, except when MNC competition is so intense that the host government has the commercial leverage to demand countertrade, or when the deal is so large—a public works project or weapons purchase—that the host country's foreign exchange cannot handle it.[27]

The host country's commercial and industrial needs are concerned primarily with business. Some are devoted to export markets. Most of the time, products get in for cash, but sometimes countertrade is required. Controlled amounts of consumer necessity items such as pots and pans, shaving cream, and some kinds of clothing are also allowed in with no quotas.

Figure 1-7.

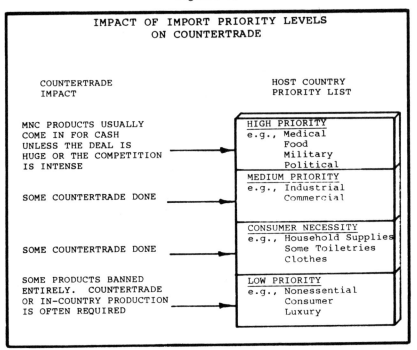

IMPACT OF IMPORT PRIORITY LEVELS
ON COUNTERTRADE

COUNTERTRADE
IMPACT

HOST COUNTRY
PRIORITY LIST

MNC PRODUCTS USUALLY
COME IN FOR CASH
UNLESS THE DEAL IS
HUGE OR THE COMPETITION
IS INTENSE

HIGH PRIORITY
e.g., Medical
      Food
      Military
      Political

SOME COUNTERTRADE DONE

MEDIUM PRIORITY
e.g., Industrial
      Commercial

SOME COUNTERTRADE DONE

CONSUMER NECESSITY
e.g., Household Supplies
      Some Toiletries
      Clothes

SOME PRODUCTS BANNED
ENTIRELY. COUNTERTRADE
OR IN-COUNTRY PRODUCTION
IS OFTEN REQUIRED

LOW PRIORITY
e.g., Nonessential
      Consumer
      Luxury

The hardest category to trade on a cash basis is the nonessential, or luxury group of imports. Quotas on these items provide the host government with a way of channeling foreign exchange expenditures away from products that do not generate more exports or increase the country's industrial or economic base. Countertrade arrangements are frequently used with this type of import. But often countries are reluctant to allow these goods in even under a countertrade arrangement.

Note that the relative strength of the dollar has a definite effect on countertrade. A strong dollar fuels U.S. companies' need for countertrade. The MNC's products are priced high, whereas countertrade goods are priced much lower. Countries feel they have to countertrade when they lack sufficient foreign exchange to purchase the products for cash. It is possible to move even poor-quality goods provided they are cheap in comparison to the dollar. A weak dollar, on the other hand, lowers the need for countertrade. In this case, the

MNC's products sell better for cash, and countertraded goods are harder to move because they become comparatively more expensive.

THE MECHANICS OF COUNTERTRADE

To understand the mechanics of countertrade, compare a representative cash and countertrade sale (Figures 1–8 and 1–9). Letters of credit and other forms of financing have been left out because they operate similarly in both cases.)

Traditionally, the MNC ships its products to a subsidiary or distributor who then sends local currency to the central bank. The central bank converts the local currency into hard currency, and the MNC gets paid. Since the 1979 oil price rise, the worldwide recession, and the international debt crisis, imports into third world countries have been restricted. This has been especially true since 1982. In some cases, like Brazil, the government may deny an import license. In other cases the central bank may refuse or be unable to convert the local currency into hard currency. Countertrade addresses these problems.

Figure 1–10 shows how a countertrade deal comes together. The upper part depicts the traditional MNC cash sales transaction and is exactly like Figure 1–9. The lower part shows how a cash export transaction works under normal free trade circumstances. The financial and legal devices listed in the middle are used for accounting purposes to link the MNC's sale with host country's export.

Figure 1–11 shows the basic mechanics of a fully assembled countertrade deal. As can be seen, the countertrade deal is a mirror transaction of the MNC's sale to its distributor.

Effectively, the countertrade in the lower half of the diagram is subsidized by the transaction in the upper half. The deal works in this manner because the producer in the third world country has difficulty selling its goods under any other circumstance. Usually the third world country's goods are too high-priced: The bottom may have fallen out of a commodities market or the goods may simply be of shoddy quality.

Because many MNCs have no expertise in moving the countertraded goods, a bank or trading firm (agent) is often hired to handle this task. In this instance, an agreement is made in advance between

Figure 1-8.

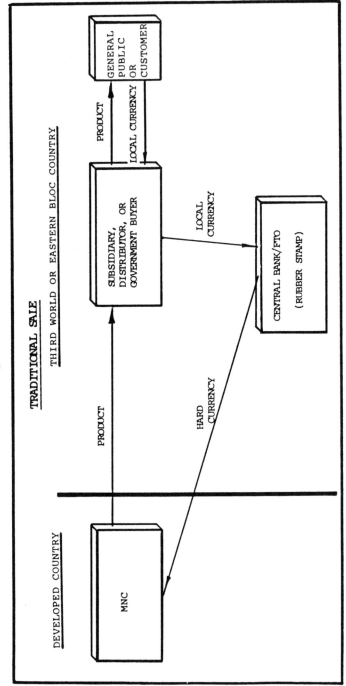

TRADITIONAL SALE

THIRD WORLD OR EASTERN BLOC COUNTRY

GENERAL PUBLIC OR CUSTOMER

PRODUCT

LOCAL CURRENCY

SUBSIDIARY, DISTRIBUTOR, OR GOVERNMENT BUYER

LOCAL CURRENCY

CENTRAL BANK/FTO

(RUBBER STAMP)

PRODUCT

HARD CURRENCY

DEVELOPED COUNTRY

MNC

Figure 1-9.

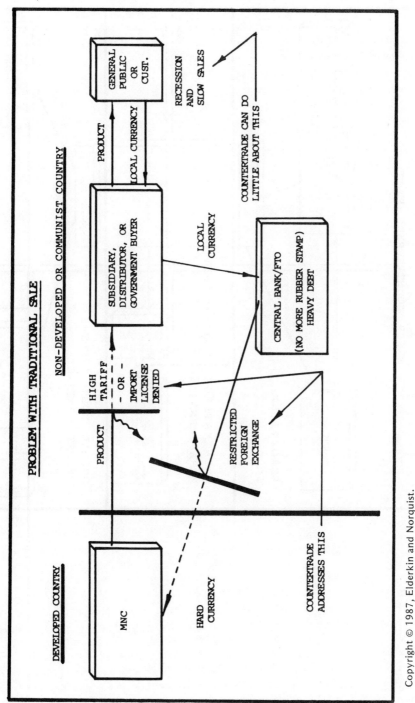

PROBLEM WITH TRADITIONAL SALE

NON-DEVELOPED OR COMMUNIST COUNTRY

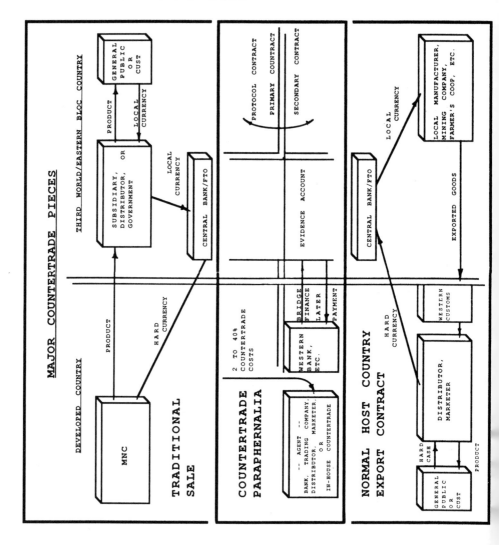

Figure 1–10.

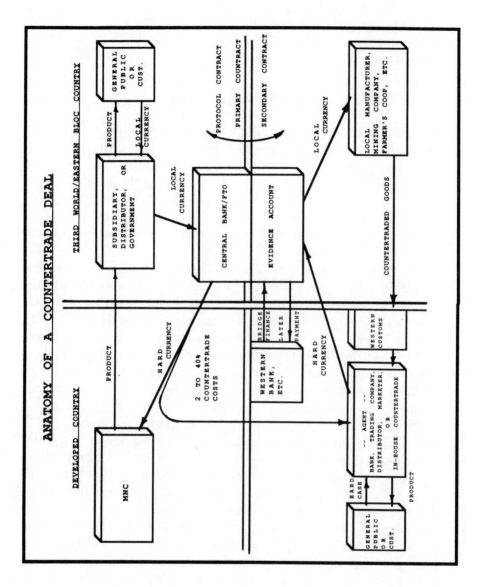

Figure 1–11.

ANATOMY OF A COUNTERTRADE DEAL

the MNC and the agent as to the terms of the trade and the cost of doing countertrade. The agent either moves the goods in the MNC's name or in its own.

THE COSTS OF COUNTERTRADE

It is important to understand that the cost to move the counter-traded goods usually includes two elements. One element consists of the fee(s) given to any outside agent(s), such as trading companies, banks, and attorneys, as payment for facilitating the deal. While fees can be expressed in daily rates, they are usually expressed as a percentage of the transaction. Fees typically run anywhere between 2 percent to over 15 percent of the amount of the purchase price of the countertraded goods.

The second part, the "discount," is the difference between the amount the MNC pays for the goods in the host country and the amount it can sell them for elsewhere, plus shipping charges, insurance, warehousing, and so forth. This cost can run between break even to 30 percent or more. Aside from attendant expenses, the cost will vary according to the ability of the MNC or its agent to beat down the price it pays for the goods, and pump up the price it gets for them. Contacts, selection of goods to be moved, and timing are of enormous importance.

Sometimes misunderstandings arise, especially when the MNC is new to the countertrade game. Banks and trading houses frequently quote only their own fees. Typically, they'll say, "We only charge ten percent to help you move goods out of country X." What they say is true. But what they sometimes leave out of their sales pitch is that the MNC may have to absorb an additional 10 to 20 percent "discount" to move the goods. Often the discount isn't mentioned for a variety of reasons: It is assumed everyone knows about it; it usually cannot be determined in advance; it might unduly frighten away MNC managers if talked about too early. So the total cost is not just the fee, as is sometimes inferred, but rather the fee plus the discount.

Therefore, any time the MNC gets a countertrade quotation, it must determine whether the figure is for the entire cost of the countertrade transaction or whether it is merely one party's fee. A request for an itemized quotation is essential.

Some maintain that countertrade transaction fees and discounts earlier amounting to 25 to 40 percent of the MNC's sale, have been in recent years reduced to as low as 7 percent. Supposedly, the greater sophistication of the world network of international traders combined with the increasing use of computers have caused the drop in costs. The figures, however, are not entirely accurate, especially for companies with little or no prior experience in countertrade. Although costs are less than what they were, the discount price varies, depending upon the relative experience and negotiating strengths of the parties involved and the market for goods taken in countertrade.

The fee for working a countertrade deal should drop as computer networks become larger and more integrated worldwide, and as business managers, government officials, and traders get more practice doing countertrade and matching transactions. A wider selection of countertrade alternatives will also bring down the discount price, but not by as large a percentage as some would suppose. Some countertrade deals are still going to entail as much as a 30 to 40 percent discount.

Some people say that if the MNC objects to a heavy discount eating away at its gross margins, it can compensate by raising prices. Many manufacturers do this, especially those with large negotiated contracts. But raising prices on a microeconomic level often is not a viable option. For one thing, it reduces sales already diminished by the strong dollar. Second, it alienates the distributor, who most often is not fooled about the higher price. Finally, price imbalances strengthen the gray market, making it even more difficult than it is already for the MNC to control the international transshipment of its products.

THE LEGAL ASPECTS OF COUNTERTRADE

From a legal standpoint, the countertrade transaction is often done with three contracts. The *primary contract* and the *secondary* (or countertrade) *contract* are like conventional sales contracts. The *protocol contract* connects the two and makes the performance of one contingent upon the performance of the other. The reason for three contracts is to lower the risk for banks, giving them additional legal recourse should the deal go sour.

With respect to contracts, there are seven major factors legal departments should consider:

1. Separation of contracts
2. Obligation to purchase
3. Penalties
4. Pricing
5. Quality
6. Distribution
7. Transferability of the countertrade obligation

The two most difficult aspects of countertrade agreements are getting the third world country's central bank to link the import license with the export license, and finding a buyer for the countertraded goods. Companies have two basic ways to dispose of countertraded goods: either use them in-house or sell them to someone else. In-house, there are four basic routes the goods can take. The MNC can use them as parts or packaging in its products; treat them as capital purchases of plant and equipment; use them for such things as premiums or company store items as non-product purchases; or buy them in bulk for a low price, use some, and pass the rest along to other MNCs at cost. Outside the company the goods can go to trading houses, bank traders, commodities exchanges, wholesalers and distributors, third parties overseas, and the U.S. government (strategic mineral reserve). Trading companies, incidentally, have expertise in both dealing with the government and distributing goods.

PURCHASING'S ROLE IN COUNTERTRADE

Emphasis in countertrade agreements in some companies is shifting from the marketing to the purchasing side of the business. The reason for the change lies in the growing importance of the purchasing department's recommendations on what to buy or how to value items offered in countertrade arrangements. In addition, purchasing might be able to establish a distribution arrangement with other MNCs, which would pass goods on at cost or slightly less. (Before the MNC does this, however, its legal department should first check with the U.S. Justice Department.)

Global sourcing, rather than global marketing, has become the new focus of attention. Companies now first search for the lowest-cost source from which to purchase, then try to get countertrade credits. Purchasing asks several questions: (1) what do their companies actually need, (2) where can those items be purchased, and (3) what source will provide the optimal package of price, delivery, service, and quality.[28]

Cost reduction, likewise, has become a major corporate goal. Sourcing from LDCs often means the MNC can lower its purchasing costs. Raw materials are cheap in third world countries and wages are low. Most MNCs have strong international positions with subsidiaries in foreign countries, as well as international transport expertise and superb marketing departments, all of which would facilitate third world sourcing.

Purchasing should first review a printout of all the items the company is buying and compare these items against what might be available elsewhere. Then it should look at items being purchased in the United States and try to determine which of these are sourced overseas and could be used to offset countertrade.

Purchasing departments should not overlook their suppliers. In some instances a considerable amount of parts and material are purchased from overseas sources. For example, Westinghouse uses over 500,000 work gloves per year. These are purchased from a three-man shop in Cleveland, Ohio. None of the work gloves, however, are made in the United States. Half are made in Hong Kong, and the rest are made in South Korea.[29]

Thus, by working more closely with these American suppliers, MNCs can extend the list of those possible things they purchase overseas. By persuading a supplier to accept countertraded exports from a country to which it would like to sell—rather than bringing them in-house directly—the MNC has expanded its range of alternatives for disposing of the exports and thus increased its chances of success. Therefore, purchasing should not only peruse its own list of purchases, but compile and review a list of its suppliers' purchases as well. This is important because so few manufacturers make product purchases directly from cash-short countries.

Using the purchasing department to help with countertrade, however, raises a number of problems. Buyers can get blamed for things beyond their control that occur in the normal course of business. In addition, they are saddled with the difficult task of keeping their in-house customers happy. Often, purchasing people are unduly criticized for taking too much time setting up third world sourcing.

It takes time and hard work to set up satisfactory, stable vendor relationships. Issues of competitive prices, merchandise quality, timely deliveries, accurate accounting, vendor contact, and in-house end-user satisfaction must all be resolved if the third world sourcing is going to be effective. Finally, there is the question of how much overall purchasing efficiency the company is willing to risk for the sake of what may be marginal sales. Third world sourcing requires breaking old vendor relationships and buying goods from unknown vendors who speak different languages, live in other cultures, and operate in different time zones. Most often they have no sales literature, nor the money to make a customer visit. In addition, sourcing goods from third world suppliers will most certainly affect a company's relationship with former vendors. Without doubt, there will be some bad feeling, especially if word gets out that the counter-traded goods are costing the MNC more than they did under the previous vendor.

For a variety of reasons it is best to maintain some contact with previous vendors. Most of the time, third world countries can supply in large quantities only a limited range of items. Developed world suppliers normally sell a much wider range of goods and offer the additional advantage of being close enough to appreciate the end-user's needs and to provide timely and efficient service.

Once the large dollar purchases are removed from vendor contracts, the company may find that volume discounts that applied across the board are curtailed. Service may deteriorate for the same reason. Just-in-time (JIT) contracts may be lost or never started. The MNC may have to buy and store several years' supply of goods sourced in the Third World in order to get immediate countertrade credits for its own sales and to guarantee its supply.

Obviously, costs must be spotted and calculated in advance in order to obtain an accurate financial picture of the corporate advantages and disadvantages of the countertrade arrangement. However, there are some hidden costs that must also be taken into consideration. For instance, what if the goods get out of spec and the MNC has to send someone to the supplier's plant located in Rangoon? What is the cost of that visit going to do to the economics of the situation?

How much time will end-users, buyers, marketing people, the countertrade manager, and company executives spend running back and forth conferring with one another about putting together countertrade deals, many of which will never be actualized? How will the time spent on dead-end deals be factored into the costs of deals that succeed? If the cost of the no-go's is not added into the cost of the successes, the MNC could delude itself into believing countertrade is worthwhile when, in fact, it is not.

How well can marketing and purchasing people, with their traditionally different perspectives, interface? The time frame of sales, for instance, is shorter than that of purchasing, as sales places importance on making this period's quota. Purchasing, on the other hand, tends to emphasize the future, trying to anticipate what can go wrong down the road.

What happens if the countertrade deal is done in a non-English-speaking country? In this case the salesperson may well be the company's primary contact with the supplier, as he or she can most easily visit the supplier during a sales trip. But once the deal is signed and the sale is made, how interested will that salesperson (paid partially on commission) be in dealing with the supplier when quality goes awry or deliveries are delayed? Who else does the buyer have to turn to when he cannot communicate with the supplier and his in-house end-user is beating him over the head?

Buyers and end-users may very well regard their participation in countertrade as a favor to the marketing department. Should they conclude they are helping marketing do its job, they are likely to ask for quid pro quo, most probably in the form of an in-house discount of their own charged to marketing to cover their purchase costs in setting up and, especially, living with the deal.

These are some of the issues that must be discussed and decided as the MNC eases into countertrade agreements. Countertrade has to be a group effort if it is to work. Acting alone, a sales group might make a commitment that could embarrass the company. According to Frank Horwitz, manager of trade projects at General Electric Trading Company, "One sure way of losing a sales opportunity or sustaining excessive risk is to expect your sales or marketing manager, skilled in his own trade of selling his product, to undertake a countertrade program, negotiate the deal, and sell his own product, all at the same time!"[30]

On the other hand, an active countertrade policy will give buyers leverage they can use in their own day-to-day negotiations. Vendors generally know who their competition is at home. But they don't know who it might be abroad, especially as new competition keeps popping up all the time. This unknown factor combined with well-timed allusions by the buyer during negotiations to low third world wage rates and international countertrade ought to be enough in certain instances to give the buyer the edge.

Upper management support and well-oiled coordination across functional boundaries are essential if countertrade is to succeed. As those in the countertrade business know so well, some of the greatest difficulties occur within the MNC itself. Therefore, it is necessary that managers understand in advance what countertrade is and how it can affect them so that they will know how to act quickly should the countertrade ball be suddenly dropped into their courts.

DECIDING WHAT TO DO

Countertrade is confusing, in part, because there are so many ways in which it can be done. Figure 1–12 is a decision tree illustrating how the MNC might go about setting up a countertrade sale. As the first step in the process the MNC must decide whether it should do

Figure 1-12.

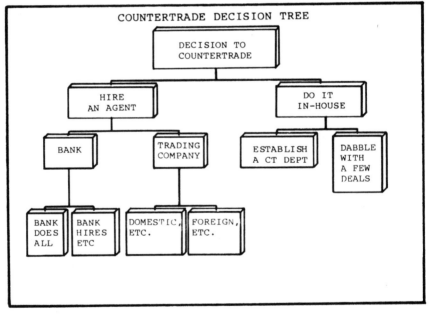

the job itself or hire an agent. As the diagram makes clear, there are a multitude of paths the MNC can ultimately take, a few of which are discussed here.

The general procedure recommended for a company thinking about its first countertrade deal is to begin by contacting a good trader, one who knows what is going on and has had experience. Even though the trader's price might be a little high, it is worth the investment. The MNC must know who the specialists are and learn how to use them and the trading companies. All corporations should have a countertrade center coordinating all its countertrade activities.

Obviously, hiring an agent requires the least involvement by the MNC. But it does cost. Handling a countertrade operation in-house offers the advantages of control, flexibility, and lower cost. On the other hand, it requires trading expertise, contacts, extensive networks, in-depth knowledge of the host country's government regulations and politics, and close coordination among departments within the MNC.[31]

A countertrade department typically overlaps into marketing, purchasing, strategic planning, and legal. Methods are being developed to integrate the countertrade department within the company. Senior level management backing is absolutely essential in setting up a countertrade department. Many MNCs are reorganizing themselves at the corporate level so that they know how trade financing and countertrade requirements affect all elements of their businesses.

The decision to handle countertrade deals within the corporation can save money and furnish valuable experience. However, it can be time-consuming and provide some unpleasant surprises. A hybrid alternative that some MNCs have chosen is to farm out the immediate countertrade needs to an agent, pay the fee, and then use an in-house arrangement to try to set up longer-term deals.

RESEARCHING COUNTERTRADE

It is the quantity, quality, understanding, and appreciation of information about the international marketplace that separates the successful companies from the unsuccessful ones. Regardless what form of countertrade a business chooses, increased information gathering and analysis are essential The relative cost of such information is the cheapest part of the international trade equation.

Today, a surprising amount of information can be found in minutes from data bases such as DIALOG, NEXIS, DOW JONES, and others. BATIS International in London has a large worldwide countertrade database, as does TRAFINEX run by Herta Siedman in New York City and IMIS headed by Dr. Alexandrides at Georgia State University. There are numerous others. The Commerce Department has its own data base as well as a considerable amount of information on countertrade and on foreign countries.[32] Companies that do not make use of relevant data bases operate partially blind. Books and periodicals form an informational base companies cannot do without. There are many English language international periodicals that give better regional coverage than those published at home.

For countertrade itself, the weekly newsletter *Countertrade Outlook* is essential. There is no other better source for up-to-date detailed information on countertrade activity around the world. *Countertrade Outlook* tells who is doing what, where, and for how much. In addition, it indicates additional sources, including books, studies, reports, and conferences about countertrade. Finally, it has a fully annotated annual listing of banks, consultants, and traders who offer their services to those needing help, complete with names of contacts and telephone numbers. Back issues, which form a wealth of research material, are indexed and still available.

Countertrade and Barter Quarterly, based in New York City, is also a must for anyone thinking about countertrade. This magazine features in-depth articles written by experts about developments in the field. Peter Harben, its editor, is one of the country's most knowledgeable persons of countertrade. It, too, keeps its readers posted on relevant events and hosts its own annual countertrade conference. Both these publications, as well as independent studies and the books published by such authorities as Pompiliu Verzariu and Leo Welt, are well worth the cost to any business investigating the potential gains of international trade.

Finally, attending countertrade conferences and seminars, meeting with bankers, traders, and consultants and traveling overseas will give businesspeople a firsthand feel for the pulse of countertrade and how it fits in with their specific needs.

NEGOTIATING COUNTERTRADE

Commercial leverage is the determining factor in any countertrade transaction. If the MNC has strong leverage, it either does not need countertrade or can get better terms. If its leverage is weak, then countertrade must be considered as an alternative.

The same is true with countries. Countries with poor balance of payments problems rely more heavily on countertrade than those that are financially sound. Countries do not want to countertrade any more than companies do. When countertrade is done, each side is making a disagreeable compromise. The company may have to subsidize the disposal of the countertraded goods once they come out of the country. On the other hand, the country has its precious export earnings tied up in products it may not necessarily want. In addition, it has to set up bureaucratic and accounting machinery to connect the import licenses with the export licenses. In this regard, countertrade will be used only when necessary.

On the seller's side, countertrade is primarily a *marketing* tool: "How am I going to sell you?" On the buyer's side, it is primarily a *financial* tool: "How am I going to pay you?"

With traditional trade, the MNC's primary market is the customer. It is the end-user who must be convinced to buy the MNC's products. With countertrade, the MNC has additional convincing to do: It must convince the government—specifically the central bank—that its products are "essential" enough to get them in.

Companies with products that do not create strong demand—*with respect to securing import licenses*—must rely more heavily on countertrade than those that do not. Because the government's needs are different from the customer's needs, a whole new marketing approach must be used. The key here is to recognize and understand the government's strategies, then to tailor the product to satisfy government requirements.

A domestic analogy is a credit policy. On the seller's side, when sales are booming and margins are high, credit is tight: "Take it or leave it." But when sales drop and margins are squeezed, credit is liberal: "Come on in and we'll see what we can do."

NOTES

1. James Walsh, "Tapping the Right Information Quickly," Countertrade Seminar, World Trade Center, New York, N.Y., December 16–17, 1985.

2. David Hurst, "Government Turns a Blind Eye as British Countertrading Blossoms," *Countertrade and Barter Quarterly* (Autumn 1984): 53–57.

3. "New Restrictions on World Trade," *Business Week*, July 19, 1982, pp. 118–22.

4. Roger Davis, "Opening Remarks," Countertrade Seminar, World Trade Center, New York, N.Y., December 16–17, 1985.

5. MNC, here, refers to any U.S. company doing business overseas. However, this report is oriented toward medium and large consumer products MNCs that sell everyday stock items rather than toward mammoth military or industrial conglomerates negotiating gargantuan deals.

6. *Countertrade Outlook*, February 4, 1985, p. 4; November 25, 1984, p. 4; July 1, 1985, p. 4.

7. "CB–Quarter Review," *Countertrade and Barter Quarterly* (Spring 1985): 8.

8. *Countertrade Outlook*, January 14, 1985, p. 3.

9. *Countertrade Outlook*, November 14, 1983, p. 2.

10. Hesham El-Abd and Michael O'Sullivan, "U.S. Military Offsets—Net Benefits or Costs?" *Countertrade and Barter Quarterly* (Autumn 1984): 50–52; "World Trade News: Countertrade Wins a Stamp of Respectability," *Financial Times*, October 25, 1984, p. 5.

11. El-Abd and O'Sullivan, "U.S. Military Offsets."

12. Philip Maher, "The Countertrade Boom: A Crummy Way to Do Business . . . But Here's How to Do It," *Business Marketing*, January 1984, pp. 50–56.

13. "New Restrictions on World Trade," *Business Week*, July 19, 1982, pp. 118–22.

14. Everett G. Martin and Thomas G. Ricks, "Countertrading Grows and Cash Short Nations Seek Marketing Help," *Wall Street Journal*, March 13, 1985, p. 1.

15. El-Abd and O'Sullivan, "U.S. Military Offsets."

16. *Countertrade Outlook*, November 11, 1985, p. 1.

17. Barry Westfall, "Countertrade—The Corporate Experience," Countertrade Seminar, World Trade Center, New York, N.Y., December 16–17, 1985.

18. Bruce Fishwild, "International Barter, Wave of the Future?" *Cedar Rapids Gazette*, April 7, 1985, p. 1E.

19. Hesh Kestin, "Trade with What?" *Forbes*, January 27, 1986, p. 33.

20. Martin and Ricks, "Countertrading Grows."

21. *Countertrade Outlook*, December 9, 1985, p. 6; May 13, 1985, p. 4.

22. Secretariat, *Countertrade: Developing Country Practices*, Organization for Economic Cooperation and Development, 1985, p. 10 (pamphlet).
23. C. B. Martin, "Countertrade—the Corporate Experience," Countertrade Seminar, World Trade Center, New York, N.Y., December 16–17, 1985.
24. *Countertrade Outlook*, April 22, 1985, p. 1.
25. Leo Welt, *Trade Without Money: Barter and Countertrade* (New York: Harcourt Brace Jovanovich, 1984), p. 97.
26. *Countertrade Outlook*, November 12, 1984, p. 2.
27. Sikorsky Helicopter sells one of the most advanced helicopters in the world. Yet because its competition is so tough, it sometimes is forced to yield to countertrade demands.
28. James Walsh, "Tapping the Right Information Quickly," Countertrade Seminar, World Trade Center, New York, N.Y., December 16–17, 1985.
29. Martin, "Countertrade—the Corporate Experience."
30. Peter Harben, "Offset: An Analytical Model," *Countertrade and Barter Quarterly* (Autumn 1984): 44.
31. David B. Yoffie, "Profiting from Countertrade," *Harvard Business Review* (May/June 1984): 8.
32. In fact, the Commerce Department is a good place for a company to begin studying countertrade, as it has done a lot of research on the subject. Both Jim Walsh, senior economist, and Pompiliu Verzariu, countertrade consultant to the Commerce Department, are resident experts in the field.

2 PUTTING TRADITIONAL COUNTERTRADE IN PERSPECTIVE
Setting the Stage

Countertrade is not a new phenomenon. International barter has been carried on for centuries. In the thirty years between 1945 and the middle 1970s Eastern bloc countries did most of the world's countertrade. The devastation of World War II, the cold war and the economic system of the socialist economies made countertrade a normal trading method. Extensive pre-war business contacts with the West—especially with Germany, with whom trade had been heavy—made it natural that ways would be found to continue to trade in spite of the political, economic, and military state of affairs after the war.

Eastern Europeans have always been good traders. Sandwiched in the middle of Europe, these nations have had goods transported through their territories for centuries. Having to negotiate with the numerous cultures around them, Eastern Europeans have always spoken a number of languages thus facilitating their skill as superb deal-makers. After the Second World War, it was natural that these people would maintain contacts and continue to trade.

Soviet hegemony and the nature of the socialist system at the end of the war encouraged countertrade. The Soviet Union did not participate in the Marshall Plan or receive other forms of U.S. aid. Short on foreign currency, lacking the incentive to make competitive products, and enmeshed in the bureaucratic turf fighting of local trading companies, Eastern European countries were forced to countertrade if they wished to trade at all.

There is no marketing system in centrally planned economies; therefore, there is no pricing system by which to value goods. Because the link between the market and production is both distant and delayed, socialist countries characteristically suffer from production shortages and overruns and products that are inferior in quality to those made in consumer-oriented societies.

The 1944 Bretton Woods agreement for thirty years assured the dominance of a wealthy United States, while countertrade remained an economic curiosity to its business community. Developed nations bought and sold for cash as did the third world nations. But by the end of the 1970s countertrade began to grow rapidly in the Third World because of rising oil prices, high debts, a worldwide recession, increased international competition, and a strong dollar.

THREE MAJOR LONG-TERM TRENDS

The growth of countertrade is the result of three major trends at work since the Second World War: production overcapacity in the developed world, the international debt crisis, and the long-term impact of technology not only on the Third World but on world trade in general.

Overcapacity

The ability of producers to make things faster than their current customers can afford to buy them is one of the prime factors motivating countertrade. Today production overcapacity runs the gamut from raw commodities to high-tech computer chips.

Overcapacity in the developed world is a relatively new phenomenon. At the end of World War II there were worldwide shortages of manufactured goods. Four of the five industrial centers (Japan, China, the USSR, and Europe) sustained significant damage in the war. This propelled the United States to a position of economic pre-eminence. In 1945 the size of the U.S. economy was fully one half of the world economy. Not only did it excel in exports in all its industries, but the United States also took a commanding lead in high technology.

By the middle 1960s, Western Europe and Japan had spent twenty years rebuilding their economies. Now they were ready to concentrate on exports and high technology. From the mid–1960s onward, the internal markets in these countries began to mature, and local industry began to compete for them more effectively.

During the 1970s, as markets in their own countries became saturated, an increasing number of Japanese and Western European companies began exporting to the United States. At the same time, manufacturing the newly industrialized countries (NICs) grew rapidly, and they began to sell increasingly on world markets.

International Debt

The second major trend since World War II pertains to international debt. The debt crisis centers around major Latin American countries and the largest banks in the industrialized world. In fact, about half the world loans outstanding are owed to the top nine U.S. banks; 85 percent of these are owed to the top twenty-five world banks.[1]

The international debt of the Third World and especially that of Latin America is closely tied to the recent history of oil prices. Until 1973 low oil prices permitted the world economy to grow rapidly. But in 1973 the world experienced not only an oil embargo, but also a fourfold increase in the price of oil, which caused a recession in the West and an imbalance in the flow of oil payments.

In the years that followed the OPEC countries began receiving massive payments for their oil. Some countries used the money for public works projects and military hardware. But the money simply came in too fast. Not wishing to lose interest on the funds, these nations deposited their money in Western banks, which then reused it to finance loans to the Third World. The banks looked upon third world countries as an acceptable risk promising a high return.

Looking back, it is hard to believe that level-headed bankers would have made many of these loans. At the time, however, the picture looked different. The growth rates of many third world nations had been strong for a number of years, interest rates were high, and the loans were backed by "sovereign" guarantees. Sovereign entities could not go broke, or so the bankers thought. If the growth rates of these countries had continued as projected and the money was used well, there would have been no debt crisis. Net foreign exchange and the growth of the GNP would have been enough to offset the size of the debts in percentage terms. Furthermore, the projected increase in foreign exchange would have been enough to cover the interest and pay down the principal, thus avoiding a turnover of loans.

Third world and Eastern bloc countries experienced a boom in economic growth in the mid–1970s. However, that growth was financed by borrowed funds. Meanwhile, in the developed world the recession wore off, industry adjusted, and the entire economic system began to grow at an unprecedented rate.

In 1979 OPEC raised the price of oil by a factor of three, thus making the price of oil twelve times what it had been at the beginning of 1973. Even more money began to flow into OPEC coffers, money that OPEC nations again could not absorb. The money went back to Western banks, which in turn reinvested it in further loans to third world countries. Only this time, the world never recovered from the oil price rise.

Inflation in the developed world was exacerbated by increased oil prices. When the economy of the Developed World slowed, demand for exports of third world commodities slackened and prices plunged. Inflation forced up prices on many products and services, especially petroleum products. High inflation led to high interest rates, and high interest rates slowed the economy.

At the same time as oil prices rose, consumers conserved to a far greater extent than experts had thought possible. Also, non-OPEC countries produced more oil. Thus, the rate of flow of dollars into OPEC accounts began to diminish. This reduced flow, coupled with the fact that OPEC countries were now spending more money on their own needs, slowed investments from these countries into Western banks.

Suddenly the flow of new loan money into third world countries was reduced to a trickle. At the same time, the recession in the developed world sharply decreased exports from the third world. Increasing amounts of foreign exchange from third world countries were needed to pay off oil imports. But, Western banks no longer were willing to extend loans beyond rolling over outstanding debts.

A number of third world countries found themselves in dire straits. Growth rates had dropped to zero. In some instances growth rates even reversed themselves and descended into negative percent-ages. Net exports dropped dramatically. Against this backdrop, inter-est payments became so large that often there was no foreign ex-change left to import the goods and services needed to invest in industry and expand exports. Additionally, instability caused massive flights of capital and decreased internal investment.

In early 1986, the price of oil slid to below $15. If it remains in this area, countertrade for some countries like Brazil might decrease as cash formerly used for petroleum is freed for other items. How-ever, countertrade by oil-producing countries may well continue due to competition. The irony is that countries, such as Iran and Nigeria that once required those who sold to them to take overpriced oil as payment, may now be asked by their customers to be paid in goods rather than cash.

Not all of the debt crisis is attributable to oil prices. A good por-tion of third world countries' problems are of their own making. Investments and loans made to the Third World in the 1970s were in many cases not effectively used. Stories abound about billions of dollars in investment and foreign aid being squandered on luxury items or siphoned back to personal bank accounts in the developed world by social and military elites. Mr. Marcos of the Philippines and Baby Doc Duvalier are but the most recent examples of this kind of activity.

European and Japanese society emerged from the Second World War with the educational and organizational talents of its people fairly intact. Third world peoples, on the other hand, begin with handicaps. They lack the pre-existing industrial base, advanced edu-cation, disciplined work force, technological skills, cohesive culture, and work and business ethic that made rapid rebuilding in Western Europe and Japan a reality.

Cultural constraints and ideology, likewise, have restricted eco-nomic growth in many parts of the Third World. This is especially true in Latin America, an area strongly influenced by socialism, cen-trality of the state, and mercantilism. Given Latin America's re-sources, these nations should be among the richest on earth. Other third world countries run by elitist governments obsessed with large industrialization projects, state control of enterprise, and oligopolis-tic industries have fared similarly. In fact, for the most part, only in those countries where the ruling classes highly supportive of busi-ness—as in the Pacific Rim—have the prospects dramatically improved. This has put the Third World in the position of being susceptible to financial distress in hard times and thus more likely to have to resort to countertrade.

Technology

The third major trend since World War II is the growing impact of technology upon trade and commerce. Technology impacts societies and economies depending upon the nature of the device and how widely it is used. Inventions in the areas of computers, transportation, and communication are becoming commonplace everywhere and have had a great impact on trade throughout the world.

Telecommunications and computers increase countertrade because they increase human interaction across the globe. They make trading easier and facilitate more complicated deals. An efficient shipping system, jet aircraft, cars, roads, and trains can move people, goods, and services over distances and at speeds heretofore not imagined. Shipping costs have declined to the point where products can be sent around the globe and sold at lower prices than identical goods produced locally.

WORLDWIDE COUNTERTRADE

No one knows exactly how much world trade is in the form of countertrade. The general consensus is that it is widespread and growing rapidly. Estimates range from 5 to 30 percent of total world trade. But a closer look reveals that most of these estimates are exaggerated and on the high side.

People who say countertrade is big usually have much to gain from promoting its growth. Most articles and speeches on the topic are done by countertrade professionals. Since the Export Trading Company Act of 1982, which allowed banks to get into countertrade, banks have energetically promoted the idea and conducted substantial marketing campaigns to create demand for their new services. In response, trading houses have redoubled their publicity efforts in order to keep the banks from stealing their traditional business.

By its very nature, countertrade has, as Fred Tarter, president of Deerfield Communications puts it, "a high baloney content."[2]

According to Edwin L. Miller, head of the MG Services countertrade London office, "There is a very high ratio of talk to action in countertrade. For every 10 or 15 deals you have proposed to you, one gets done."[3] Widespread acknowledgment of the need for countertrade has in recent years engendered inflated accounts regarding its growth and use. Countertrade is overloaded with hope, and this condition puffs its imagined size.

On the other hand, people who have nothing in particular to gain from countertrade often give much smaller estimates. Gary Banks, an economist for GATT (General Agreement on Tariffs and Trade) has made a persuasive argument for low (8 percent) figures for countertrade.[4] A recent article in the *Wall Street Journal* reported that countertraders were not doing well at all.[5] When the U.S. Commerce Department sampled a number of American executives in the fall of 1984, it was surprised to find that countertrade was actually used in Latin America less than it had expected.[6]

None of the figures given for the size of countertrade are substantiated. They are based on hearsay. Aside from the GATT assessment, no speaker on the subject, no news article, no consultant's report, no journal paper that we have seen or heard in our investigation has provided adequate documentation for its estimates.

Often researchers on the topic allow a large subjective fudge factor for "secret" deals. It is true that many companies for competitive reasons keep their countertrade deals secret.

Part of the confusion results from fuzzy definitions of countertrade. For example, there is a difference between the percentage of world trade that is *straight* countertrade and trade that *involves* countertrade, with the former figure being smaller than the latter. Bilateral trade accounts, also, are not countertrade per se. They do not link the sale of the product going into the country with the purchase of another good coming out. All they do is show a running total of debits and credits two countries have with each other. The only real countertrade involved in bilateral trade accounts is the clearing transaction at the end of the year used to balance the accounts.

Military countertrade is one of the largest types transacted in the developed world. Military countertrade is done for political reasons (job creation and technology transfer) and to prevent a sudden shift in a country's financial condition due to the size of the deals. Yet even figures for military transactions are misleading in that the countertrade usually has to be amortized over a ten- to fifteen-year period and cannot be allocated to one year.

Even if countertrade were a large element of world trade in percentage dollar terms, it would still be infinitesimally small in comparison to the number of total international transactions done per year. Ask traders how many countertrade deals they completed last year. Huge banks are lucky if they completed a dozen. Major trading houses are lucky if they did a couple hundred. The trade volume tells why. Given that total world trade is about $2.0 trillion, were countertrade to be 10 percent of the world total, that would translate into about $200 billion. Some 40 percent of the total would translate into about $800 billion. In our judgment, total world countertrade does not add up to much more than about $150 billion per year, or about the 8 percent figure the GATT estimates it to be.

In spite of the dispute as to its size, there is consensus on the following:

1. Some 200 U.S. companies are now thought to be attempting countertrade transactions.
2. About 45 companies are beginning their own countertrading companies.
3. It is generally believed that of the 155 nations in the United Nations only 20 to 30 do not countertrade.[7]
4. Around 30 countries require countertrade in certain instances.
5. Everyone agrees that countertrade is growing and that most of the growth is taking place among the LDCs.

COUNTRIES

The Eastern bloc countries have countertraded all along. Quality is sometimes poor in communist countries. Usually their goods are overpriced on world markets because they have been subsidized and because there is no direct link between the economies of East and West. Most of the available liquidity is devoted to five-year-plan purchases leaving little cash available for additional purchases. Rigid planning structures produce surpluses that need to be unloaded from time to time.

Nonsocialist countries countertrade for a variety of reasons, too. Chief among these is the need to reserve hard currency for capital goods (imports intended to generate the maximum of amount of exports) and absolute necessities (e.g., food, oil, and medical supplies). Socialist and nonsocialist countries alike often need to expand exports of goods that otherwise could not be sold abroad. Surplus commodities, undeveloped markets, poor quality, high price, and unreliable delivery create conditions under which goods will not sell abroad. Other reasons countries countertrade are:

- to hide foreign exchange from the IMF and creditors
- to get around protectionism in the developed world
- to hide commodity discounting (e.g., OPEC oil)
- to lessen the severity of government-sponsored austerity programs
- to keep from losing markets to other countries (Indonesia, for example, requires its rubber be countertraded. As a result, Malaysia felt it had to follow suit to protect its rubber markets.)

Countertrade offers a natural solution to countries trying to limit their imports and expand their exports. Since they cannot get cash for many of their goods anyway, and since they cannot afford to pay cash for non-essential imports, countertrade allows these countries to link the two together. In other words, they harness the desire of Western firms to import and use the Western firms' superior marketing expertise to increase their own exports. Yet it was not until the current debt crisis that some LDCs began looking at countertrade seriously.

In order to better approximate how various countries are countertrading, we have grouped them by region and have analyzed their activity.[8] The best place to start a countertrade walk around the world is the Pacific Rim, as it is here that a large percentage share of total world trade is conducted and rapid growth in trade is expected in future years.

The Pacific Rim

The Asian side of the Pacific Ocean includes countertrading countries listed in Table 2-1. Countries labled MNC conduct counter-

Table 2-1.

| | Reason | | Pacific Rim | | | | |
Country	MNC	TWC	Volume	CT Law	CT Policy	Resource Base	Industrial Base
Northeast Asia							
Japan	MNC		High			Low	High
South Korea		TWC	Medium	Yes		Low	Medium
China		TWC	High*	Yes		High	Low
Taiwan	MNC		Low			Medium	Medium
Hong Kong	MNC		High			Low	Medium
Southeast Asia							
Indonesia		TWC	Medium	Yes		High	Low
Malaysia		TWC	Medium	Yes		High	Low
Singapore	MNC		Low			Low	Medium
Thailand		TWC	Low			High	Low
Philippines		TWC	V Low			High	Low
Vietnam		TWC	V Low			High	Low
Australia		TWC	Medium	Yes		High	Medium
New Zealand		TWC	Low		Yes	High	Medium

*Many small cottage industry kinds of deals with Hong Kong.

trade for basically the same reasons an MNC would; other countries have objectives similar to those of third world countries (TWC). Volume is a rough estimate of how much countertrade one country does in comparison to other countries. CT Law (countertrade law) indicates whether or not the country mandates countertrade in any way; CT Policy denotes countries that simply ask for countertrade. Resource Base refers to the diversity and availability of natural resources to sustain an industrial economy. Industrial (or technological) Base indicates the extent to which a nation has developed its industrial capacity.

All major Pacific Rim countries are active in countertrade. According to the table, there is a correlation between a country's resource and technology base and its countertrade policies. While high- and medium-tech countries with low resource bases—Japan, Hong Kong, Taiwan, and Singapore—countertrade from the MNC standpoint, almost all countries with a high resource base and a low degree of technology countertrade from the standpoint of a third world country.

Of the countries that have laws mandating countertrade, all but China (which is still socialist) limit their requirements to government purchases. As far as the volume of countertrade is concerned, Japan probably ranks first due to its large economy, its voracious appetite for raw materials and semi-processed goods from third world countries, and its far-flung *Sogo Shosha* empire. China, with its record 6,000-plus buyback deals with the West for the last eight years, would probably weigh in second. Indonesia, which formerly enforced the strictest set of mandated countertrade laws in the free world, would rank third.

Within the last four years the domino effect has characterized countertrade growth in this region. While most countries became involved in countertrade for the same reasons as a typical third world country would, others jumped in as a reaction to regional competition. The Malaysians enacted their countertrade laws in part out of fear that Indonesia, with its mandated countertrade laws, would steal pieces of their rubber, tin, and oil markets. Similarly, Singapore worried that Hong Kong—which was doing most of the countertrade with China—might get a lock on that potentially lucrative market. South Korea, meanwhile, heavily in debt and short on foreign exchange, began casting a wary glance at the countertrading activities of countries like Indonesia, Malaysia, and Brazil. Thailand began countertrading to protect its traditional markets from competing countertraders. Australia has a countertrade law pertaining to military purchases. New Zealand asks for countertrade primarily as a tie-breaker between two bidders on a government contract. The Philippines would like to countertrade, but was stopped by the IMF. Vietnam does some countertrade with its Eastern bloc partners, and Taiwan countertrades by trading its manufactured products for needed raw materials.

The Indian Subcontinent

The Indian subcontinent includes the countertrading countries shown in Table 2-2. Although their countertrade activity is still low by comparison to the rest of the world, the countries of the Indian subcontinent are doing an increasing amount of countertrade. To date, India has for the most part used countertrade to balance its bilateral accounts with the USSR and a number of the Eastern European countries with which it does almost half of its trade. India has also conducted many individual deals with nonsocialist firms. Under Rajiv Gandhi's dramatic economic reforms, the government is looking for ways to consolidate and streamline the administrative process.

Burma, Bangladesh, and Sri Lanka are dabbling in countertrade, for the most part on an ad-hoc basis and with their usual trading partners. Pakistan seeks to countertrade more and more, but like the

Table 2-2.

| | Indian Subcontinent | | | | |
| | Reason | | | | CT |
Country	MNC	TWC	Volume	CT Law	Policy
India		TWC	Medium		Yes
Burma		TWC	Low		
Bangladesh		TWC	Low		
Sri Lanka		TWC	Low		
Pakistan		TWC	Medium		Yes

nations of South Korea, Malaysia, and Singapore, finds itself caught in a debate over countertrade's long-term merits.

Eastern Europe

Eastern Europe is the oldest and most frequent user of countertrade. Table 2–3 lists countertrading countries in the region.

There may be a rapid growth of East-West trade in the next several years. Formerly, East-West trade was restricted because of political and security reasons between the two camps. Two conditions are needed to increase trade: the Soviets must be assured that Eastern Europe is not going to become overly dependent on the West and the U.S. must be assured that illicit technological transfers to Eastern Europe will not be made.[9]

Because of their rigid central planning system and lack of markets to value their goods, countertrade and barter are part and parcel of the socialist way of doing business. Compared to the rest of the world, all countries of the Eastern Bloc countertrade in a major way. The amount of countertrade each does, shown above, is relative to what the others do more than to what non-socialist countries do.

Table 2–3.

	Eastern Europe				
	Reason				CT
Country	MNC	TWC	Volume	CT Law	Policy
USSR		TWC	V High	Yes	
Hungary		TWC	High	Yes	
Czechoslovakia		TWC	High	Yes	
East Germany		TWC	Medium	Yes	
Poland		TWC	Medium	Yes	
Romania		TWC	High	Yes	
Bulgaria		TWC	Low	Yes	
Yugoslavia		TWC	High	Yes	
Finland		TWC	Medium	Yes	

According to Leo Welt, President of Welt International and a leading authority on countertrade in Eastern Europe, half the countertrade done between Eastern European nations and the West is in the form of buyback.[10]

Doing business in socialist countries is far more difficult than elsewhere, and countertrade is no exception. Eastern Europeans are hard bargainers, negotiations and procedures are often slow and frustrating, and the countertraded goods are often over-priced and of poor quality.

The USSR does more countertrade than any other nation in the world. Some 70 percent of USSR countertrade arrangements involve oil and gas exchanges. Low-quality manufactured items, sold primarily to the Third World, account for the rest of its countertrade. The Soviets are primarily interested in large trade deals and are traditionally poor at dealing with marketing and customer concerns.[11]

American companies are doing business with the Soviet Union. Integrated Barter International knows a good deal about doing business there. Phibro has an office in Moscow. But it is difficult to work there. It takes longer in the Soviet Union than in other parts of Eastern Europe to get things started. However, once the Russians agree to something, their reputation is good among traders for sticking to their word. Companies are advised to first get a toehold in Eastern Europe, and then focus on the Soviet Union coming later.

Of the Eastern European countries, Hungary is said to be the most liberal for Western firms seeking to start business. Czechoslovakia is also said to be an imaginative and flexible countertrading country. Both countries are interested in trading with the West and will do what they can given the political and economic circumstances to make things work. They have close trade relationships with Viennese bankers and traders who can help facilitate deals. East Germany has a well-managed economy and does almost a third of its trade with the West. Before its economy fell in the early 1980s Poland was the second largest countertrader in Eastern Europe. Now it does much less because of the drop in overall trade.[12]

Romania is considered by many one of the most unpleasant countries in which to do business, in good part because it frequently tries to drive too hard a bargain. Along with Bulgaria (which of the Eastern bloc countries does about the least countertrade), Romania offers particularly shoddy products in return.[13] Operating within a socialist economy, but outside the Iron Curtain, Yugoslavia styles itself as a model countertrader for third world countries. However, traders complain of a number of problems doing countertrade with Yugoslavia, many of which stem from the lack of cooperation among both its trade organizations and especially its squabbling provinces. Finland's countertrade with the USSR is in recent years diminishing as Finland conducts more trade for cash with the West.[14]

Western Europe

Like the United States, most Western European countries do not like countertrade, but do it when they feel it is in their interest. As shown in Table 2-4, most Western European countries countertrade from the MNC perspective vis-à-vis the Third World and the Socialist bloc. A number of them do more countertrade than the United States because they are more internationally oriented and have colonial ties and a greater need to buy resources. Consequently, they are doing an increasing amount of trade with Eastern Europe.

Table 2-4.

	Western Europe				
	Reason				CT Policy
Country	MNC	TWC	Volume	CT Law	
Austria	MNC		High		Yes
France	MNC		High		
Italy	MNC		High		
UK	MNC		Medium		Yes
Sweden	MNC		Medium		
West Germany	MNC		Low		
Canada	MNC		Low		
Switzerland	MNC		Low		
Malta		TWC	Low		
Ireland	MNC		None		
Spain		TWC	Medium		
Portugal		TWC	Medium		
Greece		TWC	Medium		Yes

When it comes to arms trade with the United States, however, NATO countries assume the TWC stance and insist on military offsets, which constitute one of the largest percentages of total world countertrade.

Austria, France, Italy, and the United Kingdom probably are the most active countertrading countries in Western Europe. Austria does an enormous amount of countertrade as one might expect due to its proximity to Eastern Europe. However, Austria additionally does a significant amount of trade with the Third World, and soon its third world trade will outpace its trade between Eastern and Western Europe.

France is a large countertrader, with its foreign exports consisting largely of arms sales and imports of oil. Still, the French government is worried that countertraded goods might hurt cash sales should they turn up in gray markets. Italy has engaged in a number of countertrade petroleum deals, especially with Middle Eastern and North African countries. The United Kingdom countertrades when it has to in order to make the sale but asks for offsets when it makes large military purchases.

Sweden countertrades through some of its international corporations such as Volvo and Sukab, and West Germany has made a number of countertrade deals with Eastern Europe. Canada and Switzerland both do some countertrading, and Malta has dabbled in it. Ireland, on the other hand, has stayed out, preferring to stick with traditional ways of doing business.

The addition of Spain, Portugal, and Greece to the European Economic Community has created a subset of less developed countries within that organization. As members, these three countries will find their fledgling manufacturing sectors in unprecedented economic competition with the other member countries. Already, MNCs are playing a large role in Spain and Portugal as they are valued for their managerial and technological skills upgrading their production to international standards. Therefore more countertrade will probably be done there. On the other hand, third world countries may find themselves more saddled with protectionism than before, as steps are taken to safeguard the existing economies of these three newcomers.[15]

Middle East

Countertrade in the Middle East and North Africa (see Table 2-5) means the countertrade of oil. Prior to the recent drop in oil prices, as much as $30 billion of oil was being countertraded by OPEC. A number of countries such as Iraq, Kuwait, Libya, Algeria, Qatar, and Iran have avoided price structure restrictions by using oil to pay for their imports.[16]

In the past, the countertrade of oil provided a method for circumventing OPEC pricing. But with the abandonment of the OPEC quotas in late 1985, oil countertrade now provides a means for increasing market share. With the present oil glut, the countertrade of oil is similar to the countertrade of any other commodity, with the exception that oil deals can be made for longer periods of time in a well-established market.

Libya, South Africa and Kuwait have traded technological transfers—the installation of refineries—for paybacks in refined products. Saudi Arabia has done several huge countertrade deals involving military hardware. Iran and Iraq use oil to pay for all types of civilian and

Table 2-5.

| | Middle East | | | | |
| | Reason | | | | CT |
Country	MNC	TWC	Volume	CT Law	Policy
Iran		TWC	High		
Iraq		TWC	High		
Libya		TWC	High		Yes
Qatar		TWC	Medium		
Tunisia		TWC	Low		
Algeria		TWC	Medium		Yes
Egypt		TWC	Low		
Turkey		TWC	High		Yes
Saudi Arabia		TWC	High		
Jordan		TWC	High		Yes
Israel		TWC	High	Yes	
Kuwait		TWC	Medium		

military imports. Iraq has used oil to help pay for its oil pipeline through Saudi Arabia. Libya paid with oil for construction contracts from Turkey and arms from the USSR. Algeria and Turkey are using countertrade to diversify their non-oil-export sectors. Jordan primarily countertrades its major export, potash.

Israel has had mandated countertrade for all government purchases since 1967. At present, any government purchase over $100,000 is subject to countertrade requirements. Even so, the Israeli government prefers buyback deals to counterpurchases as they provide greater economic benefit.[17]

Many countries have banned trade with Israel. In spite of these and other restrictions, most notably the Arab boycott, some $500 million of Israeli goods are exported under the table to the Arabs. Through the use of numerous third parties, Israeli sales of drip irrigation systems, vegetables, and other products to Arab countries total 5 percent of Israeli exports. To keep audit trails to a minimum, much of this trade is done through various forms of countertrade.[18]

Africa

Africa has only recently begun to look at countertrade (see Table 2-6). It refrained in the past largely because of lack of government coordination, IMF pressure not to do so, some bad experiences with the Eastern Europeans, and fear of hurting cash sales. But because of its need for foreign exchange and its wealth of raw materials, Africa may well do much more countertrade in the future.

Nigeria does the most countertrade on the continent, south of the Sahara. It has engaged in a significant number of countertrade deals with several dozen countries, for the most part bartering its oil for various imports. Because South Africa trades principally with the developed world and had a strong economy, it does not need foreign exchange as much as some of its neighbors do. South Africa has no countertrade law and espouses free trade, but several companies there may quietly do deals of their own, as the country is dependent on trade. Countertrade deals disguise the origin of products, which can be advantageous for political reasons. Additionally, other countries trading with South Africa ask for countertrade in the normal course of business arrangements.

Table 2-6.

			Africa		
	Reason				CT
Country	MNC	TWC	Volume	CT Law	Policy
Ghana		TWC	Low		
Sudan		TWC	Low		
Senegal		TWC	Low		
Uganda		TWC	Low		
Namibia		TWC	Low		
Kenya		TWC	Low		
Mali		TWC	Low		
Tanzania		TWC	Low		
Zaire		TWC	Low		
Zambia		TWC	Low		
Zimbabwe		TWC	Low		
South Africa	MNC		High		
Nigeria		TWC	Medium		

Copyright © 1987, Elderkin and Norquist.

Zimbabwe has been active in countertrade in the last several years. It wants to countertrade only high-priority purchases and is careful about hurting its cash markets. Zambia has done over a dozen countertrade deals, most involving copper, its principal export. The rest of the countries listed in Table 2-6 trade various amounts of their commodity exports for manufactured items and necessities.

The Caribbean

Most Caribbean countries do not have large enough markets or enough available goods to engage in large or worthwhile countertrade deals (Table 2-7). In Mexico, however, countertrade activity has grown rapidly in the last few years and will continue to do so. With the largest GDP in the region, and with the largest debt, Mexico does the most countertrade. Because 75 percent of the country's exports are from oil, the recent oil price drop has put Mexico in dire

Table 2-7.

	Caribbean					
	Reason				CT	External
Country	MNC	TWC	Volume	CT Law	Policy	Debt
Mexico		TWC	High	Yes		97.7
Jamaica		TWC	High		Yes	3.0
Cuba		TWC	High	Yes		
Trinidad & Tob		TWC	Low			
Guyana		TWC	Low			
St Lucia		TWC	Low			
Nicaragua		TWC	Low	Yes		4.4
Honduras		TWC	Low			2.4
Panama		TWC	Low			5.1
Haiti		TWC	Low			
Costa Rica		TWC	Low	Yes		4.2
Dom Republic		TWC	Low	Yes		2.8
Guatemala		TWC	Low	Yes		2.5
El Salvador		TWC	Low			2.1

economic and political straits. Although increasing amounts of oil are being countertraded, a wide variety of Mexican products are also being exchanged for imports both on a large-scale government-to-government basis and on a private basis.

In an effort to move bauxite, its major foreign exchange earner, and to diversify its export sector, Jamaica has done a number of countertrade deals. Under Prime Minister Edward Seaga and his pro-business administration, Jamaica has in the last few years attracted almost 400 new investments, resulting in almost 20,000 new jobs.

As a socialist country, Cuba does a lot of bilateral trade with the Eastern bloc countries. But it is said that even the Cubans are unhappy with the low-quality products they get back from their communist brethren and are looking for more countertrade deals with their capitalist neighbors.[19]

The countries of Central America all do some countertrade, most of which is done on a limited basis due to the protracted war there.

In spite of the conflict, however, many Central American countries have countertraded with each other. Nicaragua does some countertrade with Cuba and other socialist countries. Costa Rica has a countertrade law but does little countertrade. Guatemala has a new law and is doing more countertrade, especially with Mexico. Panama, which still has a heavy U.S. presence, is not known to do much countertrade.

The Dominican Republic has a countertrade law and has done some countertrade deals. But, for the most part, it has refrained from additional activity because of IMF pressure. Trinidad and Tobago have done some countertrade, the major deal being a buyback of a Texaco refinery located there in exchange for the refinery's output over a number of years. Haiti has done limited countertrade on a private basis, and St. Lucia and the Grenadines have dabbled in a few small deals.

South America

There has been a rapid growth of countertrade in Latin America. Most South American countries are using countertrade to expand exports and help their private sector. As can be seen in Table 2–8, most South American countries are heavily in debt and desperate for foreign exchange.

Brazil is by far the biggest countertrader on the continent, with Colombia coming in second, only because of its smaller size. While Brazil has no countertrade law on its books, it has done many large countertrade deals through its state-run trading organizations. Much of the countertrade is with respect to oil purchases and bilateral clearing arrangements, of which the county has many. A number of switch transactions have been worked through Eastern European countries in debt to Brazil. Other deals have been done with an eye to expanding exports.

Colombia undoubtedly has the most aggressive countertrade law on the books outside of the socialist countries and Indonesia. One major object of its law is to diversify Columbia's export sector. The country has done hundreds of deals, both large and small, and with a host of other countries. Bolivia has countertraded its tin in a depressed tin market. Chile has done a little countertrade but remains strongly free-trade oriented and is in good standing with the

Table 2-8.

Country	South America Reason MNC	TWC	Volume	CT Law	CT Policy	External Debt
Brazil		TWC	High		Yes	101.9
Colombia		TWC	High	Yes		13.4
Venezuela		TWC	High			30.3
Peru		TWC	Low	Yes		13.8
Ecuador		TWC	Low	Yes		7.3
Chile		TWC	Low			19.6
Uruguay		TWC	Low	Yes		4.9
Paraguay		TWC	Low			1.9
Argentina		TWC	Medium	Yes		50.0
Guyana		TWC	Low			
Surinam		TWC	Low			
French Guyana		TWC	Low			
Bolivia		TWC	Low	Yes		3.2

IMF. Argentina has a new countertrade law and is increasingly making use of it. Peru and Ecuador countertrade foodstuffs and minerals; Paraguay is considering legislation to cover a few deals; and Uruguay has a law that asks for countertrade for government purchases.

NOTES

1. Rudiger Dornbusch, "Dealing with Debt in the 1980's," *Third World Quarterly* (July 1985): 535.
2. Fred Tarter, "Countertrade—the Corporate Experience," Countertrade Seminar, World Trade Center, New York, N.Y., December 16–17, 1985.
3. John W. Dizard, "Sears' Humbled Trading Empire," *Fortune*, June 25, 1984, p. 74.
4. Gary Banks, "The Economics and Politics of Countertrade," *The World Economy* (June 1983): 163. In 1984, GATT raised its estimate to 8 percent.

5. *Wall Street Journal*, May 24, 1984, p. 1; Dizard, "Sears' Humbled Trading Empire," p. 71.
6. *Countertrade Outlook*, October 7, 1984, p. 3. The reason cited as to why countertrade was not used more was that it was a cumbersome and difficult procedure that everyone avoided when they could.
7, Herbert Stepic, "Principal Changes in Countertrade Practice with Selected Countries after the Polish Crisis," *Countertrade and Barter Quarterly* (May 1984): 14.
8. This information has been gathered from numerous sources and is meant to provide only an approximate overview of country activity.
9. John Starrels, "EC and Comecon May Seek New Ties," *Europe*, September/October 1985, pp. 36–37.
10. Leo Welt, *Trade Without Money: Barter and Countertrade* (New York: Harcourt Brace Jovanovich, 1984), p. 119.
11. Hesh Kestin, "Trade with What?" *Forbes*, January 27, 1986, p. 33.
12. Welt, *Trade Without Money*, p. 119.
13. Ibid., p. 147.
14. Ibid., p. 119.
15. John Robinson, "Two-Speed Common Market Heading for Heavy Strains," *International Management* (December 1985): 24–30.
16. Rosemary McFadden, "The Relationship between Oil Countertrade and Energy Futures," Countertrade Seminar, World Trade Center, New York, N.Y., December 16–17, 1985.
17. U.S. Department of Commerce, *International Countertrade: A Guide for Managers and Executives*, prepared by Pompiliu Versariu (Washington, D.C.: Government Printing Office, November 1984), p. 53.
18. Hesh Kestin, "Israel's Best Kept Secret," *Forbes*, October 22, 1984, pp. 50–62.
19. *Countertrade Outlook*, November 11, 1985, p. 1.

3 MAJOR PARTIES INVOLVED

Almost two thirds of the Fortune 500 companies are involved in countertrade.[1] Some of these companies are:

Agri Industries	IBM
Avon	International Harvester
Cummins Engine	International Paper Company
Cameron Petroleum, Inc.	John Deere & Company
Chrysler Corporation	K-Mart
Coca Cola	Kinney Shoe
Conti Services	Lancaster Leaf Tobacco Company
Continental Chemical	McDonnell-Douglas
Control Data	Nike, Inc.
General Electric	Peabody World Trade Corporation
General Dynamics	Pepsico
General Motors	Sunkist
Honeywell	U.S. Steel
Hughes	Westinghouse
I.T.T.	

U.S. COMPANIES AND COUNTERTRADE

U.S. companies hate to countertrade. When they do it, it is for one reason: They want the business. It's that simple. Companies either are forced into countertrade or think they will be forced into it somewhere down the road. In almost every case companies counter-

55

trade because the conditions are to countertrade or lose the sale because of weak markets.

Motors Trading Company, a subsidiary of General Motors, moves well over $100 million worth of countertraded goods a year in over thirty different countries and has a total staff of about twenty located in Austria, Britain, Yugoslavia, and the United States. It engages primarily in offset and counterpurchase transactions rather than in buyback or straight barter deals. With the current emphasis on basic commodities, Motors Trading Company still moves a wide variety of items. General Motors itself absorbs as much of the takeback as it can through its own purchasing organization.[2]

Similarly, both Ford and Chrysler are active in countertrade. Goodyear also countertrades a number of products for its tires, including textiles, minerals, and foodstuffs.[3]

Some companies are more involved in countertrade than others. The ones heavily engaged in it usually fall into one of two classes: either they are companies with huge sales contracts (e.g., aircraft manufacturers such as McDonnell–Douglas, and chemical firms such as Dupont, Occidental Petroleum, or Allied Chemical), or they source a substantial amount of their materials internationally (e.g., large retailers such as Sears and K–Mart, or well coordinated conglomerates such as General Electric).[4]

Over thirty U.S. companies have their own countertrade departments, and about a dozen of these have set up profit centers for countertrade transactions. Several subsidiaries have offered their services to the public. Honeywell, General Electric Trading, Conti-Services, and Sears have countertrade staffs available for corporate clients.

In all countertrade situations the purchasing country either cannot or will not pay hard cash. Companies countertrade in order to:

- expand (or maintain) foreign markets
- increase sales
- sidestep liquidity problems
- repatriate blocked funds
- clean up bad debt situations
- build customer relationships
- keep from losing markets to competitors
- gain foreign contacts for future sales
- find lower-cost purchasing sources

Countertrade is rightfully seen by companies as unpleasant. Yet traders and bankers alike are often puzzled as to why large and medium-sized corporations do not perform countertrade deals when ostensibly it may be in their interest to do so.

 Unfamiliarity with and fear of the international arena are major reasons. Corporate politics may be another. Two sides of corporate politics play a role here: the conservatism of the company and the political strength of the international marketing vice president (or other company representatives favoring countertrade) vis-à-vis his or her peers and superiors.

Consider, for example, a corporation that has between $500 million and $1.5 billion worth of annual sales. It doesn't matter, really, whether it is a manufacturing or a service enterprise. But let's say it does have a good network of international subsidiaries and distributors and derives a substantial part of its sales from foreign customers. The corporation is, then, no stranger to international business. Why doesn't it countertrade?

Suppose foreign sales are off a bit and the president is interested in them. The vice president of international marketing, (we'll call him Mr. Veep) is doing the best he can to pull them up. Say, the corporation cannot get its blivets into Colombia because Colombia deems them "nonessential" and will not provide the necessary import license.

Suppose Mr. Veep finds out that the blivets can be countertraded into Colombia through a third party who exchanges them for, say, locally produced buggy whips, but for a 20 percent discount and fee ($1 million). Let's assume that after looking around, Mr. Veep decides this is the best he can do within the immediate future. Suppose the gross margin on the blivets is about 25 percent. So Mr. Veep has a choice: to countertrade and take the hit or lose the sale.

Mr. Veep goes ahead with the countertrade deal and moves $5 million worth of product into Colombia. At the next meeting when he makes the announcement that a $5 million sale had been made, everyone smiles. But when it becomes known that $1 million had to be paid to get the products in, faces fall. Instead of being praised as a hero for creatively solving sticky international liquidity problems, Mr. Veep becomes the object of vigorous attack. Forget about maintaining market share in Colombia. Forget about contributing to overhead. From the standpoint of many executives, Mr. Veep did not make a $5 million sale; he "lost" the company one million dollars.

Suspecting the products have actually been sold for $4 million instead of $5 million, the vice president of domestic marketing demands a guarantee that the same products will not wind up on domestic shelves in the gray market. Corporate counsel muses out loud whether or not the company will be subject to future dumping charges coming through the government from the buggy whip industry in the United States. He's heard, he says, U.S. buggy whip manufacturers are flat on their backs, mad as hell, and not going to take it anymore.

"What do you mean by that?" asks the president.

"Oh, you know," answers counsel, thoughtfully smoking his pipe. "The usual thing. They'll tell the attorney general we're subsidizing foreign imports that are being dumped in the U.S. market and hurting domestic industry. We don't know exactly what kind of legal action they might take—enjoining or suing us—or whether or not they will actually block the importation of the whips. But we may have to get our outside counsel in Washington involved."

"I know that they can make a hell of a PR fuss," chimes in the public relations vice president. "I can see it now. TV news shots inside the buggy whip plants of philosophical old men, who have been there since the beginning of time, assembling the things. Cut to people punching the clock for the last time after being laid off. Close-up of the fat lady's face inside her trailer a half a mile away. Tears well in her eyes as she wonders what she and her family are going to do now, with no job. Mike Wallace knocks on our door demanding to know how we could be so heartless and hurt our fellow Americans in the name of profit and greed. Oh yes. It's a 'juicy story,' as journalists like to say."

"But we're selling the whips to Hungary," answers Mr. Veep defensively.

"It doesn't make any difference," responds the vice president of finance. "I read in the *Journal* several days ago that the buggy whip market is weak right now. I doubt that Hungary is big enough to absorb $5 million worth of buggy whips. They'll probably redistribute a large part of the shipment elsewhere. That forces down the world buggy whip price even further. Even if they don't actually arrive on U.S. shores, if word gets out about this deal, the U.S. buggy whip industry could still make its point: American export firms are hurting their own neighbors by subsidizing foreign competition."

Brows furrow and heads shake.

The president turns to Mr. Veep, looks him straight in the eye, and says through his teeth, "I don't want trouble."

Now suppose Mr. Veep says "no" to the trader and refuses to make the sale. At the next meeting the president turns to him and asks how international sales are doing. At this point, Mr. Veep responds with a short speech. "The international world is in tough shape," he says. "The dollar is still too high and spendthrift nations have run up huge debts. Compared to other international companies, our company is doing well."

"No, Mr. President," Mr. Veep goes on, "there is no dramatic increase in sales from last week. We had an offer from a trader to get our blivets into Colombia in exchange for buggy whips on one of those countertrade deals. But he wanted an arm and a leg. He asked for a 20 percent fee. I couldn't get him down. Can you believe that? I told him he was crazy!

"I've done some studying about this countertrade stuff. Quite honestly, Mr. President, I think there is a hell of a lot of risk in any kind of countertrade deal. If that deal had gone sour, we may have lost the whole $5 million.

"No, we didn't make it this time. But we're investigating all avenues so that as soon as there is an opening, we'll seize it. Oh, by the way, Mr. President, you'll be pleased to know our sales are up in West Germany."

This time lips purse and heads nod around the table. "Good thing we have such a prudent international marketing vice president," people tell each other later on. "Yes Sir. It really sounds like there are a lot of sharks in the international marketplace. Good thing we're in such good hands." Thus, internal politics wins the day and a possible sale is lost.

Yet, regardless of the corporate culture, no company is entirely free of politics. Because of this few corporate executives move with as free a hand as traders. Corporate decisions are made by committees, not individuals. While committees tend to blunt brilliance they do lower the blunder rate, which is a major reason for their existence. It is blunders, rather than an absence of brilliance, that get executives fired the fastest. Thus, the inside political risks of countertrade often loom far larger in an executive's mind than the outside financial risks.

Frustrations of Countertrade

Countertrade is a highly frustrating endeavor. Many deals fall through. Two major difficulties businesspeople encounter are an inability to market the countertraded goods and failure to obtain the government approval necessary to complete the deal.

In regard to marketing countertraded goods, the Electrolyzer Corporation from Canada got a surprise on its first countertrade deal made a year or so ago. After selling a hydrogen generating plant to an East European country, the company received what its spokesperson called, "an unspecified grab bag of goods," consisting of yachts, rubber gloves, and electric motors.[5]

In order to cover the high administrative costs of setting up a countertrade deal minimum costs run around $2 million. Most countertraders do not like to go below this figure, as it is not worth their while—unless they can piggyback one countertrade deal onto larger deals.[6] Of late, however, there have been countertrade arrangements in the $100,000 per transaction range, but deals like these are still few in number.[7]

Another reason why the dollar figures for countertrade are large is that many countertrade exchanges involve commodities coming out of the host country. These goods are easy to grade for quality and can always be sold because they have ready markets. But the profit margins can be slim; thus, the most efficient shipping methods must be used. Even so, unless the deals have government backing, commodity-to-commodity exchanges seldom work. The reason for this is that the commodities coming in have too slim a margin to support the loss taken on the commodities coming out.[8]

Countertraders charge larger discounts for manufactured goods because of the higher risk involved with selling them. Barry Westfall, vice president of ContiTrade Services, reflects the skepticism of many traders in regard to taking value-added products. In his view the incremental production capacities of most third world firms cannot provide enough business to make the countertrade deal worthwhile. Only with commodities can business get into the million-dollar-plus category quickly.[9] Unlike commodities, manufactured goods can carry the additional risk of cultural singularity, inferior quality, and shipment damages.

But even commodities can get traders into trouble. Renault made a mistake a number of years back when it took coffee beans in exchange for cars. Rather than trying to sell the beans to a commodities broker, Renault thought it would try its hand at a little cooking and converted the beans into what ended up being a huge batch of lousy-tasting instant coffee which had to be thrown out.[10]

MNCs selling a small amount of goods to a large number of countries can have difficulty making countertrade agreements work to their advantage. Ideally, many small countertrade transactions would best suit their needs. But most of ten smaller deals are not economical to set up.[11]

There are other problems with countertrade. Language barriers, mistaken cultural assumptions, long distances between producer and market, international boundaries, and the number of parties involved in the transaction cloud information and communication. In addition, with the exception of a few firms, U.S. corporations generally lack expertise in dealing with countertraded goods.

Establishing a meeting of the minds among the involved parties up front can be tricky. Participants have differing needs and will suggest conflicting solutions for problem areas. Finding a common ground requires patience and timing. Some deals dissolve when Western banks refuse LDCs the bridge financing required when the buy and sell deals are several months apart.

Range of Outcomes

Examples of countertrade deals run the gamut from the good, to the bad, to the bizarre. First, the good:

Good	Pepsi Cola sells Pepsi syrup to its plant in Romania in exchange for wine, which it then sells through its distribution systems in developed countries. (Even so, it had to get its wine bottles from Hungary.)[12]
Sweet & Sour	Sweet: McDonnell-Douglas sells planes to Poland in exchange for canned ham, which it serves to its employees for lunch in its cafeterias.
	Sour: Reportedly, McDonnell-Douglas employees are tired of eating ham!

The quantity of ham involved is not known. But think how much ham would have to be exchanged for even one DC-10. That's quite a bit of ham![13]

Bad   GTE takes telephone rotaries out of Poland as part of a countertrade deal there. Evidently, the rotaries meet technical specifications. Yet GTE deliberately scraps the entire lot. Reason: the rotaries delivered were pink, chartreuse, and orange.[14]

Bad   Fiat opens a plant in the Soviet Union for cars to be made and sold in Eastern Europe. Suddenly, it finds the cars being sold all over Western Europe at a substantial discount. Problem: The contract did not say the Soviets could not sell the cars outside of Eastern Europe, and the Soviets evidently wanted the hard currency more than the cars.[15]

Imaginative   In an effort to induce a West German auto manufacturer to sell it automobiles, the government of Mongolia offered to sell it a 150 million year-old dinosaur skeleton. The Germans politely declined.[16]

THE FEDERAL GOVERNMENT

What does the U.S. government think about countertrade? Secretary of State George Schultz reportedly said, "Countertrade is a communist way of doing business and the U.S. government won't get into it!"[17] In fact, because no one government department or agency has overall authority over countertrade, and the administration has not seen fit to take a hard stand, what the U.S. government really thinks about countertrade varies depending on which part of the government one talks to. As might be expected, the view of each federal agency with any opinion on the matter reflects that agency's internal concerns and whether it feels countertrade will help or hurt it. Here's the lineup:

Department	General Opinion	Major Concern
Agriculture	Yay! Yay! Yay!	Moving surplus foodstuffs
Commerce	Yay!	Expansion of exports
Congress	Nay	Dumping and unfair competition
Customs	Nay	Harder valuation
Defense	Yay/Nay	Helps arms industry/Security problems

Department	General Opinion	Major Concern
IRS	Nay	Fewer audit trails
Int'l Trade Comm	Nay	Erosion of free trade
Labor	Nay!	Lost jobs from imports
Secretary of State	Nay! Nay! Nay!	Erosion of free trade
State Department	Nay, but maybe yay	Does it hurt/help U.S. policy?
Treasury	Nay	Erosion of free trade

The U.S. Department of Agriculture is strongly in favor of counter-trade because it wants to move its food surpluses. Such foodstuffs as corn, wheat, nonfat dried milk, cheese, barley, and sorghum are now sitting in storage bins around the country, a result of past efforts to maintain agricultural commodity prices. At the same time, there is the belief that the nation has a deficit in its strategic materials reserve. The United States could obtain cadmium from South Korea; fluorspar from Mexico; rubber from Indonesia; and cobalt, chromite, and titanium from Zambia, Algeria, Zaire, and the Philippines. So a number of the farm states—led in part by Congressman Byron L. Dorgan from North Dakota—have been pushing for countertrade deals in which excess American foodstuffs are traded for strategic raw materials to supplement the reserve.[18]

Even so, the administration has vacillated on working more countertrade deals. It has executed only a few deals, one of which was an exchange of nonfat dry milk for Jamaican bauxite. Supporters charge that the administration is ideologically hung up on free trade. But opponents fear that the large-scale bartering of foodstuffs for strategic raw materials would depress world food prices and thus hurt U.S. farmers even more.[19]

Although it is not in favor of mandated countertrade, the Commerce Department is interested in doing anything it can to expand U.S. exports and understands that countertrade is an important competitive tool. Located in the Commerce Department's International Trade Administration, economist James Walsh and trade expert Pompiliu Verzariu advise companies about countertrade. Mr. Walsh handles the broad aspects of the subject, and Mr. Verzariu helps with the details of specific deals. These gentlemen feel that countertrade is growing and is here to stay.[20]

Congress is examining countertrade from the standpoint of dumping and unfair competition and their impact on the United States. It is also looking into U.S. technology transfer to the Third World and elsewhere as a means of preserving the technological edge of the United States.[21] Congress has not reacted well, however, to U.S. allies requesting offsets when they purchase U.S. arms. Nor has Congress liked mandated countertrade by other countries. In the last three years, the U.S. government has given $5 billion in aid to Mexico and Brazil to help those nations through their debt crisis.[22] Why, critics ask, do U.S. exporters lose sales to these countries because they couldn't meet the countertrade requirements when U.S. tax dollars are being used to purchase them in the first place?

Since the Camp David Accord, Egypt has received $15 billion in U.S. aid. Israel now gets $3 billion per year. But all of these nations ask for countertrade. Some members of Congress call it "triple dipping,"—once for taxes subsidizing R&D, which often is not included in the price of the product; once for providing military aid and pumping money from U.S. bases located abroad into local economies; and once for carrying the disproportionately high burden for other nations' defense systems, especially nations in Asia. What enrages some members of Congress is when a country buys a small quantity of high-tech American arms, disassembles them, adds improvements, and then competes by selling their upgraded version on the open market.

The Customs Department is interested in countertrade because it wants to place a value on imports coming into the United States and keep sensitive technology from being exported to the wrong end-users. Recently, customs investigated Soviet, Iranian and Libyan oil being dumped in the U.S. market.[23]

For the past decade, the Defense Department has actively helped U.S. arms dealers make international sales through countertrade transactions. As Defense Department thinking goes, the more countries buy U.S. arms, the more they are allied with the United States. In addition, countertrade allows American military suppliers to amortize some of their costs on overseas sales and induces nonmilitary purchases from the United States. As of late, however, the Defense Department has been concerned about countertrade's impact on national security. Yet the unauthorized proliferation of military technology is as much a function of a coming shakeout in the world arms industry as countertrade, which is a vehicle of trade.

The IRS is interested in countertrade from the standpoint both of money laundering and tracking transactions. The Labor Department worries about the imports induced by countertrade eliminating U.S.

jobs. The Treasury Department is concerned about making financial transfers conventionally. In addition, the Treasury Department supports multilateral trade, and since countertrade tends to be bilateral in nature, Treasury is not in favor of countertrade. The U.S. Trade Representative also supports multilateral trade and is afraid countertrade will erode it. The State Department, naturally, is the most politically motivated. It likes to present the public image of strict adherence to GATT standards but will help with countertrade if it suits its foreign policy objectives.[24]

At the top of this pyramid is the administration, which is vulnerable to intense criticism no matter which way it turns. So, it tolerates countertrade. It wants to maintain the free trade system but realizes that exports must be increased. Despite the existence of opposing viewpoints, many in government feel that not much can be done on an official level to stop or even slow significantly countertrade activity.[25]

Legislation

During the 1970s the United States experienced a decline in its international competitive position. For each succeeding year there was a net deficit in the nation's balance of payments.[26] By the end of the decade, domestic stagnation and high unemployment were widespread. In their search for remedies lawmakers learned a number of things.

Exports are extremely important. They account for 11 percent of U.S. manufacturing jobs. But America had not kept pace with global trade. The U.S. share of world exports dropped from 18 percent in 1960 to 12 percent in 1980. But the potential for expanding exports was there. Of over 250,000 U.S. manufacturers, 90 percent did not export. Of the 25,000 U.S. manufacturers that did export, 100 companies accounted for 50 percent of the export volume, and 250 companies (1 percent of all U.S. manufacturing firms) accounted for 80 percent.[27]

Economists estimated another 25,000 small and medium-sized manufacturers could profitably export if given some help. This would boost total U.S. exports to 5 percent within five years. But a lack of financial backing, the time and personnel to devote to international sales, and the economies of scale needed to spread international risks prevented these firms from exporting. Additionally, they lacked experience and expertise in the following:

- Foreign market evaluation
- Customs regulation
- International finance
- Foreign exchange transactions
- Documentation
- Shipping
- Packaging[28]

Traditionally, U.S. antitrust law has taken a dim view of countertrade. Prior to the 1982 Export Trading Company Act, the Sherman Antitrust Act prohibited export trading firms from servicing manufacturers. Banks, likewise, were barred from international trading by the Glass-Steagall Act of 1933. It is not inexpensive imports that raise objections. It is rather the belief (sometimes justified) that these imports are being unfairly subsidized by someone else's exports. Specifically, opponents fear the dumping of foreign goods on U.S. markets, which, in turn, hurts domestic manufacturers.[29] Behind antitrust law is the philosophy that export and import transactions should be kept separate.

Antitrust proponents presume that MNCs have been coerced into taking countertraded goods. These goods are perceived as coming into the country at marginal prices, slowing domestic production, reducing capital reinvestment, and eventually making the nation dependent on this new outside source. Once dependence is effected, the foreign producer is in a good position to charge monopoly prices at the consumer's expense.

Antitrust people look closely for distortions in purchasing decisions supposedly made on the basis of competitive factors—low price, high quality, and good service. Countertrade may force a purchasing department to overlook these criteria and buy low-quality, high-priced goods in order to sell its own company's products. Decisions such as these can make it impossible for domestic (?) vendors to compete. Countertrade raises many antitrust issues; therefore, it is recommended that companies get a good international attorney to handle the government.

The Export Trading Company Act was intended to expand U.S. exports by permitting the formation of trading companies that would help exporting manufacturers. Specifically, it encouraged more financing by allowing banks to own and run their own trading companies.

Experts believed that export trading companies would provide all needed services in a one-stop package. And U.S. banks, already highly sophisticated and deeply involved in international finance, could provide advice and financial backing[30] and thus light the way. In addition, the act was intended to allay exporting companies' fears by loosening antitrust interpretations of statutes and having the Justice and Commerce Departments issue advisory antitrust opinions (called certifications) in advance.[31]

Those MNCs wishing to ensure against being charged at a later date with violating the Sherman Antitrust Act could obtain prior governmental certification releasing them from subsequent suit. The certification is made by the Secretary of Commerce in concert with the Justice Department. Before the certification is issued, a determination is made as to whether or not the transaction will:

1. Substantially lessen competition or restrain trade within the United States
2. Not unreasonably alter prices of U.S. goods or services similar to those being exported
3. Not constitute an unfair method of competition against U.S. exporters of similar products
4. Not allow the exported goods to find their way back to the United States.[32]

Although well intentioned, the Export Trading Company Act of 1982 has several major weaknesses.[33] One weakness is that it is limited to export trade. Imports are not covered and still come under the old antitrust rules. By limiting itself to export trade this law goes only half way. Trade is a two-way street. Goods and services have to come back sometime or exports will grind to a halt. Countertrade recognizes this. The 1982 Export Trading Company Act does not.

In order to compete effectively against foreign firms, export trading companies have to be able to deal in third country trade, trade not necessarily related to U.S. exports. In order for them to establish strong contacts and trading flexibility, they have to be able to operate on both the import and export side of third country trade. Otherwise, non–U.S. trading companies will always have an advantage. This is the export company's fundamental dilemma: balancing the need to export with the need to limit imports.

In addition, The Export Trading Company Act employs a cumbersome and slow certification procedure, which may well stymie the export activity of small and medium-sized companies. Antitrust implications of tied sales still have a chilling effect on U.S. business.

Many feel that seeking certification is not worth the time and effort. In the first place, the Justice Department refuses to be bound by its own opinion. It reserves the right to rethink decisions later on. Second, the department takes a good deal of time to issue an opinion to begin with, thus causing the loss of potential sales. Third, even if the Justice Department were to stand by its decisions, if the company does not follow every article of its original proposal to the letter, the advisory opinion is regarded as worthless. Finally, simply requesting an advisory opinion increases a company's profile with the Justice Department, which, in turn, makes it more vulnerable to subsequent legal attack.[34] The upshot is that, legally speaking, it still does not pay to touch the U.S. Justice Department, unless one wants to sue somebody else.

Another objection is that the act creates a private claim whereby one American export company can use it as a device to directly sue an American competitor for "unfair methods of competition." Allowing one U.S. company to sue another in an American court for grievances suffered in foreign markets overreaches American court jurisdiction. Worse, it can add uncertainty to exporting, the very thing the law seeks to avoid.

The irony is that U.S. businesses have more domestic freedom than business in most other countries but much less international freedom. It should be noted that U.S. law is not accepted in foreign countries; however, under certain circumstances arrangements can be made in which foreign governments will accept the results of arbitration conducted in a neutral country such as Switzerland.

Trade both to and from the United States is covered by the same federal statutes. It is easier to get exports than imports through customs, however, unless they are stopped, for national defense reasons, at the request of another government or because the administration or Congress wants to embargo sales to some country. Despite the presence of powerful U.S. interests—unions and beleaguered manufacturers—who do not wish to see a rise in imports, legislation is needed that will give U.S. trading companies a free hand abroad.

There are other federal statutes that impact countertrade to a lesser degree. The Foreign Sales Corporation (FSC) is a new type of entity that has been devised under the Deficits Reduction Act of 1984. This new law allows corporations to defer some of their overseas profits to avoid paying tax on them.[35] This can give the MNC a little more time to structure a countertrade deal, as no one likes having to pay taxes on funds they can't use.

The Trade Act of 1974 lets the president establish import quotas, increase tariffs, reduce imports from communist nations, retaliate against the unfair trade practices of other countries, and negotiate orderly marketing agreements with the advice of the International Trade Commission.[36]

The Trade Agreements Act of 1979 has provisions that place antidumping duties on goods priced below fair value (cost of production) and impose countervailing duties on imports that have been subsidized by foreign governments. It also lays out the manner in which imported goods should be valued to determine *ad valorem* (percent of value)-based customs duties. Normally the value is set at the cash exchanged, since most transactions are goods for cash; however, countertrade transactions can be difficult as they are complex and subject to various interpretations. In order to stave off both conflict and unwelcome surprises a major consideration in the implementation of both laws must be the degree to which the imports are hurting domestic industry and commerce.[37]

BANKS AND EXPORT TRADING COMPANIES

A number of American banks have expanded their traditional services to include countertrade. The larger ones are:

Bank America	Citibank
Bank of Boston	First Chicago
Chase Manhattan	Manufacturers Hanover
Chemical Bank	Security Pacific

Banks of other nations are also involved in countertrade. Austria has been a focal point of countertrade for some time. The Central Bank of Vienna is a big countertrader, as well as numerous others. Because of the U.K.'s colonial contacts, its proximity to Europe, and its attraction to Arabs, who prefer setting up banking and business offices there, London is rapidly becoming a countertrade center. There are four large British banks doing countertrade: Barclays, Lloyds, Midland, and National Westminster.[38]

Countertrade is not a central function of banks. Bank trading staffs tend to be small, and a number of countertrade departments have lost money. Some banks, such as European American Bank, have removed themselves from countertrade activity altogether. Countertrade departments are viewed primarily as a method for rounding out a portfolio of banking services in order to attract traditional banking business.

Banks, then, are more facilitators than traders. Very few actually countertrade themselves. They are good at advising as to how countertrade should be done and who should be used as an agent. Banks can conceptualize the transaction, put the buyer in contact with the seller, do various kinds of research, and help finance the deal. However, they are not as good at the details of countertrading as are the countertrading houses.

Before the Export Trading Company Act of 1982, banks could not trade at all. Reactions by banks to that act have ranged from enthusiastic to lukewarm. There are 1400 commercial banks in the United States, and only a couple dozen of them have set up export trading companies.[39] Banks with worldwide networks of branch offices, or whose senior officers are internationally oriented have been the most active.

One of the reasons why some banks welcomed the 1982 Export Trading Company Act was that they saw in it a way of using their newly-formed trading departments to countertrade themselves out of loan exposures to debtor nations. Given that Citibank's Latin American loans of over $4 billion, for example, are larger than its net worth, there has been some thinking about this possibility.

While banks do not like taking title to goods or taking trade risks, old-line trading houses nevertheless have felt threatened by their countertrade initiatives. Traditional countertraders have become defensive and critical about banks and in large measure see them as stealing some of their turf. Countertraders are vulnerable to competition because they charge high prices, and banks use price competition to gain an advantage.

Countertraders say that banks are not as on top of the trade picture as are trading companies. Trading companies supposedly are talking directly to buyers and sellers all the time. Bankers reportedly hire countertraders but use them primarily in administrative and sales roles. Banks moreover, do not buy and sell as often as do large trading companies. Neither do they have as large a specialized countertrading staff. Therefore, say the trading companies, the banks do not have as sharp an edge.

Thus far, banks have been more consultants than traders. But as they develop their staffs and their contacts they should do more countertrade. Some predict banks may be the leading export intermediaries of the late 1980s and the 1990s. The large banks already have vast organizational infrastructures in place around the world that they can use to facilitate countertrade activities. In addition, they have in-depth international financial expertise. It is the potential of banks, rather than their present activity, that worries traders the most.

International Trade Certificates

The amount of time and effort needed to get the paperwork through third world government bureaucracies and central banks for approval is a major problem area in countertrade. Each of the 170 nations of the world has a unique set of laws. Simply keeping track of changes in world law could fill volumes. Therefore, countertrade, as well as international business in general, must deal with the problems of the standardization of laws, regulations, and procedures.

An international uniform commercial code—hammered out in a multinational treaty signed by the major trading countries and similar to the one used in the United States—would be ideal as international commerce continues to increase. Such a code will take time in coming, however. In the meantime, smaller steps are being taken to standardize countertrade as much as possible.

Parallel technical banking agreements (PTBA) are being used increasingly in Eastern Europe offset agreements along with special trading arrangements (STA). The PTBAs facilitate coordination between the central banks of the two countries when bilateral trade clearing accounts are established. They make sure that the accounts in the two banks are mirror accounts of each other. PTBAs are really to be used only for large clearing accounts with a minimum balance of $10 million and normally over $50 million.[40]

In another attempt toward trade standardization, Chase Manhattan and the Bank of America World Trade Corporation in Brazil are buying and selling East European trade credits. These run about 10 to 11 percent of the value of the MNC's sale, depending on the country and the products. Their use, however, is thus far limited to specific countries.

Clearly the most ambitious attempt to date to standardize the countertrade process has been made by David Cookson at the Bank of Boston's International Trading Services Group in New York City. With the conceptualization of the idea by Hector Caram-Andruet, president of General Foods Trading, the Bank of Boston is attempting to persuade a number of different countries to accept the newly developed International trading certificate (ITC).

The ITC is a certificate that the MNC wishing to export its products into a participating country buys from the Bank of Boston. The certificate will allow the MNC to make the sale without the hassle of having to take anything in countertrade. Effectively, in a countertrading world, it is the next best thing to selling for cash. The genius of the ITC is that it performs the countertrade function in reverse. In other words, goods are taken out of the host country before the product is shipped in. This means that the country has cash in hand from its exports before it purchases the MNC's products.

Here's how it works. A company in the developed world purchases something from a participating host country that it might not have purchased before. The company makes the purchase for cash on the condition that it be given an ITC for all or a percentage of the value of the goods bought. The ITC is a guarantee by that country's central bank that the negotiated amount of hard currency is available on demand to an MNC exporting there, provided that its products are on the ITC's list of possible products to be imported.

Next, the developed world purchasing company either sells or transfers its ITC to the Bank of Boston, which places it in its "ITC Exchange." The Bank of Boston then looks around for companies trying to export to that particular country those things on the ITC's list, companies that would otherwise be forced to countertrade in order to get their exports in. When it funds such a company the bank sells the company the ITC. In the third step the company presents the ITC to the host country's central bank, gets permission to ship its products, and gets paid in hard currency. Figure 3–1 shows all the steps combined.

Because it is a negotiable instrument, the ITC standardizes the documentation process and is targeted principally for new and incremental exports. It saves the exporting company advertising and distribution expenses as well as administrative costs. Finally, it is of

Figure 3-1.

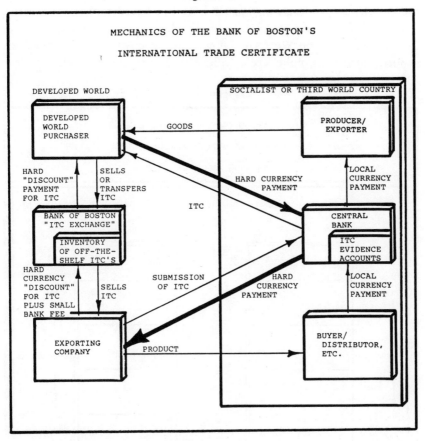

MECHANICS OF THE BANK OF BOSTON'S

INTERNATIONAL TRADE CERTIFICATE

greatest use when the exporting MNC and the entity taking back the goods are independent parties.

The ITC is intended to increase exports from the host country, simplify and speed the counterpurchase requirements for a Western exporter, make countertrade a documentary form of trade, increase administrative efficiency, reduce the Western exporter's risk, increase the exporter's success ratio, and multilateralize international trade. By keeping exports and imports as separate as possible, it eliminates entirely the necessity that manufacturers trade goods about which they know little. By providing central bank backing, it increases the confidence level of those looking to trade, and hence increase trade in general.[41]

The ITC could also be used to help clearing accounts in bilateral and reciprocal trade arrangements between governments. All parties in the process would stand to gain. The host country increases incremental exports, the Western buyer reduces costs, and the Western exporter is able to make a relatively worry-free countertrade sale.[42]

Figure 3-2.

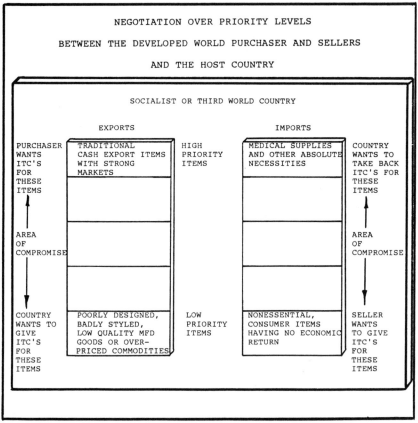

Naturally, there is going to be maneuvering by the original purchasing company and the host country as to the kind of deal that is struck. Much of the negotiation will be over the relative priorities each party places on imports and exports (Figure 3-2). As the illustration shows, the host country is not going to want to give ITCs for exports it could make for cash. Nor is it going to want to include those imports on any ITC list of nonessential items. The host country will want to trade its less-desirable exports for high-priority imports.

Conversely, the purchasing company will want to get ITCs for otherwise routine cash purchases and have all kinds of possible nonessential imports placed on the list so that it will appeal to a larger number of MNCs wishing to sell goods there. The greater the demand for the ITC, the greater its price. On the other hand, if the host country restricts its list too much, the purchasing company might not be able to sell the ITC at all, thus lowering its incentive to make repeat purchases.[43]

At present, the ITC is being examined by Eastern European and Latin American countries, where the Bank of Boston has extensive contacts. Unfortunately, the Bank of Boston and General Foods have been unsuccessful in eliciting interest in the ITC in a number of countries. Several European countries have given the concept a less than enthusiastic reception, however.

Governments may wish to maintain control on an individual transaction basis rather than giving what appears to be blanket authority to someone else to set up the transaction. They may have trouble organizing and monitoring the system on a bureaucratic level. Also, governments might not believe they have enough countertrade to warrant the cost of setting up the system. Finally, such an arrangement might not create that much in the way of exports or new buyers, and there is always the chance it will cannibalize cash sales.

Some resistance may be due precisely to the ITC's attractiveness. Countertraders may not like it because it could mean that the Bank of Boston would take away some of their business. Western banks may see it as a threat to their business interests as well. Then, too, because the idea is new, it takes time for people to get used to it, overcome bureaucratic inertia, and get over the nobody-wants-to-be-first syndrome.

Regardless of its merits, then, the backers of ITCs have their work cut out for them. But they may be close to success. Venezuela has taken an interest in the concept, and Czechoslovakia has already worked two ITC deals. If the People's Republic of China, which had the concept presented to its financial and trade officials in the winter of 1986, were to adopt it, then the ITC would definitely be on its way to success.

EXPORT TRADING COMPANIES

European Trading Companies

Export trading companies, of course, have always been in business. The oldest ones are based in Eastern Europe, as modern countertrade originated there after World War II. These trading houses are well established entities in East–West trade. In fact, it has been claimed that the best countertraders are people who have grown up in Eastern Europe, as they are intimately familiar with Eastern European culture, political, and economic systems; speak many languages fluently; and are supremely practical, alert, and wary.[44]

One trading company doing extremely well is MG Services. Launched in 1983 as a 50–50 joint venture between Metallgesellschaft, a huge West German commodities firm, and Louis Dreyfus, a large French financial house, this firm did $150 million worth of countertrade business in its first six months of existence and because of its aggressiveness and low fees is rapidly becoming a highly respected trader on the world scene.[45]

Japanese Trading Companies

There are a total of 8,000 trading companies in Japan. Although the Japanese have been active at countertrade for centuries, these modern companies did not begin to grow until the late 1940s and 1950s. As the Japanese economy recovered from the war, intermediaries were needed to trade Japanese manufactured products for raw materials.

The sixteen largest Japanese trading companies are called *sogo shosha*. There names are:[46]

C. Itoh & Company, Ltd	Mitsui & Company, Ltd
Chori Co, Ltd	Nichimen Company
Itoman & Co, Ltd	Nissholwai & Company, Ltd
Kanematsu–Gosho	Nozaki & Company, Ltd
Kawasho Corporation	Okura & Co, Ltd
Kinsho–Mataichi Corporation, Ltd	Sumitomo Corporation
Marubeni Corporation	Toshuku, Ltd
Mitsubishi Corporation	Toyo Menka Kaisha, Ltd

The *sogo shosha* are highly diversified. They deal in 25,000 different products in every country in the world. Together, they employ 81,000 people. They have worldwide communications networks and extensive and highly effective information-gathering services. Activities of these trading companies include:

- Brokering between buyers and sellers
- Marketing and distributing goods
- Organizing large business and government projects
- Offering strong financial assistance
- Providing excellent marketing research and investment advice
- Facilitating the progress of joint ventures

In Japan, the *sogo shosha* handle 65 percent of the nation's imports, 55 percent of its exports, and 33 percent of its GNP. Mitsui and Mitsubishi alone handle about 10 percent of Japanese exports to the United States.[47]

The origin of most Japanese trade companies, at least the larger ones, was as a trading arm of other companies wishing to sell their wares overseas. In 1900, Japanese trading companies handled over one-third of Japan's trade. By the end of World War I, they handled four-fifths of their country's trade. The companies grew to substantial size in the 1930s, but they remained under control of powerful families. After World War II, they were broken up but subsequently regrouped under public and various kinds of private ownership.[48]

Japanese *sogo shosha* plan to be a major vehicle enabling Japan to make major investments beyond its borders. According to the 1983 Mitsui Annual Report, Japan's investment overseas is expected to rise markedly in the coming years.[49] Some major trends in this direction include:

1. The expansion of existing ventures as opposed to starting new ones
2. Increased investing in manufacturing and financial houses in North America and loans to South East Asia, but decreased investments in Oceania and the Middle East
3. A shift away from investments in pulp, paper, and chemicals toward investments in transportation, equipment, and electrical machinery

The *sogo shosha* are not without their weaknesses. Much of their commodity sector is of low profitability, and this problem is compounded by the disinclination of the Japanese to divest themselves of those businesses. The staffs of the *sogo shosha* have not been especially good at strategic planning, although this is improving. When it comes to moving countertraded goods, the *sogo shosha* have just as much difficulty distributing them as others do. Large potential corporate customers bypass their services, preferring in-house marketing units similar to those found in U.S. corporations. The *sogo shosha* are not positioned well to capitalize on new technologies. Some Westerners feel they are financially overextended and undercapitalized.[50] (Japan's approach has had strong influence in both Korea and Brazil. Both of these countries have gone on to launch their own successful versions of the *sogo shosha*.)[51]

American Trading Companies

American export trading companies did not begin until the late 1950s and 1960s, because the American economy was so strong in those years there was no real need for them. In fact, they did not begin to grow until the end of the 1970s. Some of the larger trading companies doing business in the U.S. are:

American Ace	Miteo/Mid American
Boles World Trade Corp	International Trading Company
Conti-Services	Noble Trading Company
Fleet Financial	Philipp-Salomon
General Electric Trading	Sears World Trade, Inc.
I.B.I.	Sime Darby Commodities
International Commodities Export	Univex
M.G. Services	Vine Associates
Mitsubishi Corporation	

Countertrade is a contact and knowledge business. Trading companies are strong because they have spent years developing both. They have large staffs, extensive networks of contacts, and expertise gained from years of practice. Many are able to quantify costs and risks up front. For instance, Phibro—considered one of the best in the business—will even assume the risk in advance.

We have seen some of the differences between traders and bankers. But there are differences between traders and countertraders, too. As opposed to traditional trade, where there may be hundreds, even thousands of traders in a firm, there are only a few people in the countertrade office. Countertraders have to be generalists, spreading themselves over a wide variety of products, engaging in laborious and slow decision-making processes, and arranging deals that may take months or years to complete. Traders, on the other hand, are specialists. Traders work with a set line of commodities or products that they get to know intimately. They make quick decisions about deals that can take only minutes to come to closure.

The driving force behind traders is to make a profit moving the goods. The driving force behind countertraders is to help with financing or help a client seeking to increase sales. Traders deal with a small network of other traders around the world who are also specialists in specific commodities. They know each other, and the mechanisms of trade are well established. Countertraders deal with a large network of people with whom they do not often interact, or who are sometimes total strangers.

In countertrade, the mechanism for how the deal is to be transacted must be created each time. Traders rarely deal with government people, and when they do, the government representatives behave as though they were working for private companies. Politics are rarely their concern. Countertraders deal with government people all the time, and with countertrade, politics can be a major concern. Traders complete numerous deals, sometimes many a day. Countertraders complete very few deals.[52]

In addition to traders, there are about 300 barter exchanges in the United States, only a few of which are international in scope. Exchanges differ from barter dealing, where each deal is worked individually. In an exchange, companies become members of an organization, often by paying some kind of membership fee and agreeing to barter goods and services with the other members. Supposedly, unusable assets and hard-to-move inventory are to be traded for such things as airplane seats, promotional services, and advertising space. It isn't an easy business. The weakness of barter exchanges is that members want more to unload their own slow-moving merchandise than they want to buy anyone else's. In addition, IRS auditors are suspicious of barter transactions and insist on knowing the equivalent market value of the items traded.[53]

In the past year there has been a shakeout in the countertrade industry. A number of companies, banks, and trading firms have reduced their staffs. UNIVEX, a barter exchange launched with much fanfare, has fallen on hard times and delayed opening its international barter operation. Sears World Trade has cut back its operations substantially. The countertrade units of the J. Henry Schroder Bank and Trust Company, and the European American Bank have closed. In the middle of 1985, Boles World Trading Corporation filed for Chapter 11. Those who remain in the countertrade field will do so because of their skill, their large infrastructures of networks, and their ability to carve out their own particular market niches.

Costs of Traders

Many traders maintain that countertrade deals cost between 5 and 7 percent of the value of the MNC's product sold. Then news stories appear about deals costing 15 to 40 percent. Why the disparity?

One reason is confusion between the trader's fee and the total cost of the transaction. Another is that some deals are more difficult to work. Certain countertraded goods are easier to move than others. This means a lot when the discount is determined. Some countries are easier to deal with than others. In certain instances, everything goes smoothly. This, in turn, lowers the cost. In other instances, the reverse is true.

There is another less well-known aspect of costing countertrade deals. Large MNCs doing large billion-dollar countertrade deals can get lower prices than companies that only occasionally dabble in countertrade. For instance, large companies like GE, Sears, General Motors, or Westinghouse can afford to have their own full-time staffs trading for them and even setting up trade organizations for them. Staffs such as these can marshall tremendous resources. They have extensive networks of contacts and data bases telling what can be traded where. They can work large deals and thus force down the percentage discount and fee. Finally, when circumstances require it they can threaten to take their large volume of business elsewhere.

Enter the smaller company wanting to export its products into a country that will not issue the necessary import licenses. Lacking extensive contacts in the international community, the small company must cold-call banks and trading firms. Generally it has a more difficult time than large companies shopping around. The small company has to be told what countertrade is and how it works. It doesn't know who is good in the trade and who is not, who is strong in the country in question and who is not. Most traders are not enthused about doing a $0.5 million deal, and their trading chutzpah often persuades them to make the bid high, especially if they know the company is uninitiated and not likely to need their services again. For the small company the costs of transacting a countertrade deal can run high. When people talk about total costs of 5 to 7 percent, keep in mind this many times represents what they will finally agree to, but often not the figure they will start with.

By working with good countertraders, companies can avoid the mess of having to make countertrade arrangements themselves. Even so, there are drawbacks.[54] Countertraders are expensive. Some are reputed to make over $1 million per year in commissions. Countertraders make their money off the manufacturer (the MNC), not the customer. Finally, because there is no standardization of fees charged by trading companies, there is little way of knowing how much countertraders should be paid.

It is wise to shop for separate countertraders for different types of transactions. No trading company is large enough to manage effectively one-stop trading around the world. Most of them specialize in product groupings or geographic locations. This specialization can skew the advice they give. In certain instances, they recommend what is best for them rather than what is best for the client.

Trading companies are made up of people who are traders. They can set up complicated and imaginative deals. But they deal in established goods. They may overlook creative uses of traditional goods such as alterations, new packaging, or new market applications. They may not be innovative—or helpful at all—with intangible products such as services.

Countertraders are primarily brokers. They connect sellers with buyers. Sometimes they are good at finding available products but cannot find markets for them. Unless someone is willing to take the product, countertraders are ill prepared to establish a market from scratch.

LAW FIRMS

There are a number of good U.S. law firms with expertise in international trade. Some of them are:[55]

Arnold & Porter	Washington, D.C.
Fleischmann & Farber	San Francisco, Calif.
Ginsberg, Feldman, Weil & Bress	Washington, D.C.
Heller, Ehrman, White & McAuliffe	San Francisco, Calif.

Hughes, Hubbard & Reed	Washington, D.C.
Kantor, Davidoff, Rabbino, Wolfe & Kass	New York, N.Y.
Lane & Mittendorf	Washington, D.C.
Lecomte, Barber, Emanuelson, Tick & Doyle	Boston, Mass.
McGuire, Woods & Battle	Washington, D.C.
Milbank, Tweed, Aadley & McCloy	New York, N.Y.
Oppenheimer, Wolff, Foster, Shepard & Donnelly	Minneapolis, Minn.
Patton, Boggs & Blow	Washington, D.C.
Steptoe & Johnson	Washington, D.C.
Verner, Lipfert, Bernaard & McPherson	Washington, D.C.
Wald, Harkrader & Ross	Washington, D.C.

A number of law firms are experienced in countertrade and can offer valuable advice. Attorneys are good negotiators. They can also help avoid snags with the government when the time comes to bring home the countertraded goods. Many law firms have overseas offices and contacts with attorneys in LDCs. Working through these networks, potential wrinkles with the foreign governments can be ironed out in advance.

The disadvantage of law firms is that they are expensive and can complicate and slow the process so much so that they scare off the other party. Occasionally, lawyers can be so intent on avoiding contractual risk that the deal never goes through. Contingency clauses may so complicate the arrangement that the other party loses interest.

Vis-à-vis much of the world, Americans have a unique attitude toward the law. When writing a contract, Americans try to anticipate all the ways it can go wrong and cover themselves in advance. In contrast, other nationalities cover the main points in the contract and assume that the rest will work. If things do not work and there are problems, they assume that ways will be found to solve them.

When Americans begin to enumerate all the ways the contract can fail, they can give non–Americans the impression that Americans are overly bureaucratic or untrustworthy. Non–Americans doing business with Americans for the first time often feel weighted down with a lot of unnecessary legal detail.

Even in America, if you have a dispute with someone and contact your lawyer it's tantamount to calling up the tanks. But in the United States bringing in the tanks is standard procedure. We are a litigious society.[56] Bringing in the lawyers or filing a suit in an international transaction, however, can have altogether different consequences. Such actions are taken much more seriously in other societies. Other nationalities expect negotiating parties will hash out their differences among themselves, even if justice suffers somewhat in the process. American companies fighting each other bitterly in court can still be doing business together. Filing a suit against a foreign company usually means an end to future business relationships, as other nationalities take suits much more personally than do Americans.

Negotiating involves leverage. There are two types of leverage in a contract: legal leverage and commercial leverage. Both are designed to keep the other party on the hook—to make it more advantageous to cooperate than to cut and run. Legal leverage says, effectively, "If you don't do what you agreed to do in the contract, I'll get a court to make you pay me damages." Commercial leverage says, "It is more in your interest to abide by the contract, because I have a piece of the action you don't have but need to make things work. In other words, you can't make as much money if you don't have me." Legal leverage is strong when the contract is signed and carried out by Americans entirely within the United States. Legal leverage is weak—or non-existent—when the contract is international. In this case there is no legal entity with jurisdiction over both parties to enforce the contract.

Commercial leverage includes acts that may hold up one party's performance until the dispute is settled.

Fortunately, steps can be taken to assure strong commercial leverage. Internationally, it may be the only leverage a company has. While lawyers can offer good advice on commercial leverage, the executive has the primary responsibility. In the end, it's best to get as much leverage as one can.

INSURANCE COMPANIES

Several insurance firms cover countertrade, and their business is said to be tripling every year.[57] Some of them are:

AIG Political Risk, Inc.
Alexander & Alexander
American Countertrade & Export Association
Chubb

Continental Insurance
INA
Investment Insurance International Managers, Ltd
IPAC
Lloyds of London
Travelers Insurance
Virginia Center for International Trade

Alexander and Alexander Services, Inc., the second largest international insurance brokerage company in the world, provides a broad range of risk management and financial services to all kinds of clients. AIG Political Risk Division (AIGPRD), affiliated with the National Union Fire Insurance Company of Pittsburgh, Pennsylvania, and CIGNA World Wide, affiliated with AETNA Insurance Company, both handle countertrade. The Foreign Credit Insurance Association (FCIA) is made up of an association of private insurance companies that underwrite deals made by the EXIM Bank of the United States, a public corporation of the U.S. government. FCIA Insurance restricts itself to exports from the United States. All three companies will insure default brought about by either political or commercial circumstances.

Insurance companies cover a number of types of risk, including:

1. Export license revocation
2. Import license cancellation
3. Various official acts of either the buyer's or seller's governments that would negatively effect the contract
4. Termination of the contract (e.g., non-performance)
5. Civil war, riots, rebellion, etc.
6. Interruption of shipping
7. Cancellation of export credits
8. Product guarantee
9. Product liability[58]

Companies are advised to insure while the countertrade deal is still in its conceptualization stage because, as Mr. Boylan, international insurance expert at Alexander and Alexander Services, cautions, "No one insures a burning building."[59] Most of the time, insurance is available but sometimes it is not. Phibro got insurance for a 4.5 percent premium when it exchanged machinery for Dominican cocoa, but when Unilever tried to sell $12 million worth of soap to Romania, the deal fell through because Unilever could not get adequate insurance.[60]

Most insurance for countertrade covers political risk related to the hostile act of a government that frustrates business activity. Normally, the insured is covered from the time the countertrade transaction is started until the time it ends, because often the sale into and the purchase out of the host country do not occur simultaneously. Examples of insurable political risk include the confiscation of American-owned property with Castro's coming to power in Cuba and the Ayatollah Khomeini in Iran.

Political risk covers the actions of public entities but not that of private parties. The insurance contract changes dramatically depending on whether the parties to a countertrade transaction are public or private entities. A public entity is defined as a central government or one of its agencies, a provincial government, or a public or state corporation. Usually, political risk is limited to specifically defined politically oriented causes of loss. An act or omission of a policyholder that results in a loss is normally not covered. Unless otherwise stated, issuance of international insurance policies are governed by the rules of Lloyds Underwriters.

The terms of the contract will indicate whether the insurance covers only political risk or both political and commercial risk. Commercial risk occurs when banks or companies in third world countries cannot pay or when there are devaluations of currencies, exchange fluctuations, transfer risk, and disputes. The essential difference between the two types of risk is the presence or absence of hostility aimed at the business transaction itself. Often when commercial risk is excluded, it is excluded entirely.

Normally, political risk does not include breach of contract. Insurance can cover breach of contract and force majeure conditions. A few insurance companies, including EXIM Bank, AIG Political Risk, and CIGNA, will cover defaults of private sector obligors. Under certain conditions, the Export–Import (EMIX) Bank of the United States is to guarantee facilities on a government-sponsored basis. Lloyds definitely does not want to handle commercial risk.[61]

Insurance companies lean toward repetitive commodity transactions. They avoid specialty products and transactions that take more than a year to complete. AIG Political Risk asks a minimum premium of $50,000 per contract.

NOTES

1. Robert Blumel, "Buying or Selling, Barter Is Becoming a Booming Alternative to Cash," *Purchasing World*, March 1985, pp. 78, 80.

2. Philip Maher, "The Countertrade Boom: A Crummy Way to Do Business . . . But Here's How to Do It," *Business Marketing*, January 1984, pp. 50–56.

3. Everett G. Martin and Thomas E. Ricks, "Countertrading Grows and Cash Short Nations Seek Marketing Help," *Wall Street Journal*, March 13, 1985, p. 1.

4. General Electric is one of the most diversified companies in the world. It manufactures and is involved in services in 340 of the 400 basic SIC categories.

5. *Countertrade Outlook*, October 17, 1983, p. 2.

6. Mitsui, a Japanese *sogo shosha*, will consider doing countertrade amounting to between $500,000 and $1 million. Mitsui is offering lower countertrade threshold deals to attract a wider clientele.

7. *Countertrade Outlook*, December 10, 1984, p. 1.

8. Barry Westfall, "Countertrade—the Corporate Experience," Countertrade Seminar, World Trade Center, New York, N.Y., December 16-17, 1985.

9. Ibid.

10. Jane Rippateau, "Countertrade Activities in the Auto Industry, Part I Europe," *Countertrade and Barter Quarterly* (Spring 1985): 41–43.

11. However, one of the smallest countertrade deals ever to be considered is the $9,000 sale of fiberglass boats and bathtubs from the Dominican Republic for $7,000 of an undisclosed party's nail polish remover. And one of the smallest completed countertrade deals was the export of $44,,000 of Dominican Republic toilet bowls to American Standard in exchange for toilet tank accessories for about the same amount. *Countertrade Outlook*, November 18, 1985, p. 4.

12. *Countertrade Outlook*, November 7, 1983, p. 1.

13. Maher, "The Countertrade Boom."

14. *Countertrade Outlook*, November 14, 1983, p. 1.

15. Robert E. Weingand, "Barters and Buybacks: Let Western Firms Beware!" *Business Horizons*, June 1980, p. 60.

16. Gary Banks, "The Economics and Politics of Countertrade," *The World Economy* (June 1983): 160.

17. *Countertrade Outlook*, October 9, 1983, p. 2; January 21, 1985, p. 4. Mr. Schultz's feelings are understandable. A Bechtel spokesperson stated, just after Mr. Schultz left that company's presidency to become secretary of state, that, "The only compensation we want is money." Clearly,

Mr. Schultz came from a company dead-set against countertrade. "New Restrictions on World Trade," *Business Week*, July 19, 1982, pp. 118–22.

18. Peter Harben, "Congressman Sees Barter Ameliorating World Hunger. . . . If the Administration Doesn't Miss the Train," *Countertrade and Barter Quarterly* (Autumn 1984): 22-26.

19. Ibid.

20. James Walsh, "Tapping the Right Information Quickly," Countertrade Seminar, World Trade Center, New York, N.Y., December 16-17, 1985.

21. *Countertrade Outlook*, July 29, 1985, p. 1.

22. Hesh Kestin, "Trade with What?" *Forbes*, January 27, 1986, p. 33; *Countertrade Outlook*, June 24, 1985, p. 1.

23. *Countertrade Outlook*, June 10, 1985, p. 3.

24. "New Restrictions on World Trade."

25. "Growing Worries over Buyback Deals," *Chemical Week*, June 2, 1982, pp. 36–43.

26. In 1984, for the first time since 1910, the United States was a debtor nation, as its cumulative current account balance slid from a break-even point at the end of 1983 to more than a $100 billion deficit. Within the span of one year, the United States took on more international debt than the nations of Mexico or Brazil took during the past decade.

27. Gurvdutt M. Baliga and Harold R. Williams, "The U.S. Export Trading Company Act of 1982, Nature and Evaluation," *Journal of World Trade Law* (May/June 1983): 224.

28. Ibid.

29. Thomas B. McVey, Esq., "A Legal Review of Countertrade Transactions," *Countertrade and Barter Quarterly* (May 1984): 57.

30. Baliga and Williams, "Export Trading Company Act."

31. Donald Zarin, "The Export Trading Company Act: Reducing Antitrust Uncertainty in Export Trade," *George Washington Journal of International Law and Economics*, no. 2 (1983): 300.

32. Joseph P. Griffin, "Antitrust Law Issues in Countertrade," *Journal of World Trade Law* (May/June 1983): 236.

33. Ibid., p. 245.

34. Mitchel Rabbibo, "Legal Requisites of Countertrade," Countertrade Seminar, World Trade Center, New York, N.Y., December 16-17, 1985.

35. Patrick Giles and Thomas B. McVey, "Countertrade as a Tax Planning Debice," *Countertrade and Barter Quarterly* (Winter 1984): 72-74.

36. Donald Zarin, "Countertrade and the Law," *George Washington Journal of International Law and Economics* 18, no. 2 (1984): 235-95.

37. Ibid.

38. Henry Cooke, "UK Banks and Countertrade," *Countertrade and Barter Quarterly* (Spring 1985): 24-25.

39. Peter Harben, "U.S. Banks—The New Traders on the Block," *Countertrade and Barter Quarterly* (Summer 1984): 9–12.
40. *Countertrade Outlook*, October 21, 1985, p. 2.
41. David S. Cookson, "International Trading Certificates—A Multilateral Reciprocal Trade System," *Journal of the Institute of Export* (July/August 1985): 18; David S. Cookson, "The ITC Association: A Proposal," Bank of Boston, Fall 1985 (brochure).
42. Cookson, "International Trading Certificates."
43. Ibid.
44. John W. Dizzard, "The Explosion of International Barter," *Fortune*, February 7, 1983, p. 91.
45. "Metal Market: MG, Dreyfus Countertrade Giant Formed," *American Metal Market*, December 3, 1984, pp. 17, 21.
46. Sogo Sosha Committee, "The Sogo Sosha: What They Are and How They Can Work for You," Japan Foreign Trade Council, January 1984, p. 8 (pamphlet).
47. Ibid.
48. Ted Dickson, "Japan's Merchant Elite—the Sogo Shosha," *Countertrade and Barter Quarterly* (Winter 1984): 55–58.
49. Mitsui 1983 Annual Report, p. 6.
50. Richard T. Koskella and Donna M. Nemer, "The Sogo Shosha—Can They Adapt, Can They Survive?" *Countertrade and Barter Quarterly* (Winter 1984): 61–64; Yasuo Oki, "Countertrade and the Japanese Sogo Shosha," *Countertrade and Barter Quarterly* (Winter 1984): 58–60.
51. Baliga and Williams, "Export Trading Company Act."
52. Chuck Martin, "Corporate Experience in Countertrade," Countertrade Seminar, World Trade Center, New York, N.Y., December 16–17, 1985.
53. Robert Blumel, "Buying or Selling, Barter Is Becoming a Booming Alternative to Cash," *Purchasing World*, March 1985, pp. 78–80.
54. *Countertrade Outlook*, January 18, 1984, p. 2; January 23, 1983, p. 1.
55. Philip Maher, "The Countertrade Boom," p. 56.
56. Jethro K. Lieberman, *The Litigious Society* (New York: Basic Books, 1981).
57. Michael Hughes, "Opening Remarks," Countertrade Seminar, World Trade Center, New York, N.Y., December 16–17, 1985.
58. *Countertrade Outlook*, various issues.
59. Francis X. Boylan, "Trade Finance Political/Export Credit Risks," Bankers Association for Foreign Trade, Center for International Banking Studies, Key Biscayne, Fla., February 11, 1985 (speech).
60. *Countertrade Outlook*, April 29, 1985, p. 3; October 21, 1985, p. 1.
61. Boylan, "Trade Finance Political/Export Credit Risk."

4 RESISTANCE TO COUNTERTRADE

Third world countries believe that countertrade helps them strike better bargains and expand their net exports. At the present time countertrade often does just this. Since MNCs wish to trade in cash, they have been slow to recognize this benefit of countertrade.

However, countertrade can cause problems. It cannibalizes the cash sales of countries that engage in it on a regular basis. For countries that countertrade imports, countertrade increases their price. It induces developed world companies to demand countertrade from third world countries, and, at the same time, causes the developed world to become more protectionist. Finally, it reduces total world trade because it locks in bilateral restraints, raises transaction costs and risks, and makes international trade so complicated that some businesses drop out entirely.

CASH SALES ARE HURT

Cannibalization of cash sales is harmful to third world countries dependent on one or two primary products such as oil, bauxite, rubber, coffee, etc. Most countertrade done with these primary exports is on a short-term, ad-hoc basis. Countertrading countries often have to import most other goods because their local industries are small and not diversified. This means that large swings in the commodity prices of their primary exports can have devastating effects on the domestic economies of countertrading countries. Countertrade is sometimes used to try to lock in markets in order to stabilize volumes and prices for the medium and long term, rather than to get the compensation in cash.[1]

Sometimes countries get burned directly on their cash sales. A while back, several companies wishing to sell to Mexico purchased all the domestic honey they could find to generate the foreign exchange needed to maximize their sales there. The Mexican honey producers were ecstatic, but not for long. Unable to move the honey at the price they had originally intended, the foreign companies dumped it in Mexico's traditional cash honey markets, depressing the price of honey, and costing the Mexican honey exporters over the long term. The Mexican honey producers' complaints, as well as those of other Mexican businesses, have made the Mexican government extremely wary of allowing countertrade to encroach upon its traditional cash markets.[2]

Yet even when countries search for the *incremental* customer in an effort to ensure that countertraded goods do not hurt their cash sales, the gains can be illusory. If the market is depressed and inelastic, the "new" countertrade customer is usually some other nation's cash customer (Figure 4–1).

In this regard, countertrade is little more than disguised price cutting. It cannot expand a market for an inelastic commodity. A domino effect ensues in which country A steals market shares from country B in year one; country B steals market shares from country C in year two, etc. Once it starts, countertrade is hard to stop. Over time, it shifts the exports of the participants from cash sales to sales in which the proceeds are earmarked and raises the cost of the imports received.

Malaysia, for example, got into countertrade primarily because it feared Indonesia, a competitor in oil, rubber, and several other products, was using countertrade to steal the Malaysian market share. Singapore, similarly, suspects that Hong Kong already has trade with China wrapped up as a result of its more than 5,000 countertrade deals with China.

Countertrade and bilateral clearing accounts can produce political embarrassments as well. Recently, Pakistan told Kuwait, Saudi Arabia, and the United Arab Emirates that it wanted them to take

Figure 4-1.

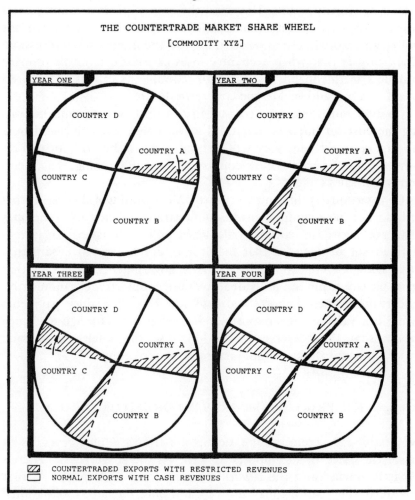

THE COUNTERTRADE MARKET SHARE WHEEL
[COMMODITY XYZ]

YEAR ONE — COUNTRY D, COUNTRY A, COUNTRY C, COUNTRY B

YEAR TWO — COUNTRY D, COUNTRY A, COUNTRY C, COUNTRY B

YEAR THREE — COUNTRY D, COUNTRY A, COUNTRY C, COUNTRY B

YEAR FOUR — COUNTRY D, COUNTRY A, COUNTRY C, COUNTRY B

COUNTERTRADED EXPORTS WITH RESTRICTED REVENUES
NORMAL EXPORTS WITH CASH REVENUES

more of its products through countertrade. Oman soon asked Pakistan to purchase more Omani oil to compensate for an Omani trade deficit attributable to Oman's purchases of Pakistani textiles, garments, and rice. Pakistan agreed to the Omani request, but to do so Pakistan must decrease its oil purchases from Saudi Arabia. Saudi Arabia, needless to say, is not happy about this.[3] To make matters worse, because Pakistan is buying its oil elsewhere, Iran has significantly reduced its purchasing from Pakistan.

The incremental exports from a country's own countertrade efforts are highly visible. However, the cash exports a country loses because of a competing country's countertrade sales are often not visible and more likely to be attributed to the international recession. The irony is that when a country loses cash exports on its primary products in this manner, it tends to redouble its efforts to countertrade, and just add fuel to the countertrade fire.

Countertrade lowers the costs of third world exports while increasing the costs of imports. But third world countries are afraid if they do not countertrade, they will lose sales. What they do not realize, however, is that when other countries do the same thing, they themselves lose sales.

Countertrade is difficult to control. Most third world governments still do not have comprehensive countertrade policies. Even the ones that are active in countertrade leave policy decisions to a well-defined set of agencies that monitor trade and try to ensure that cash sales are not cannibalized. Many governments are afraid that local private firms and individuals will use countertrade fraudulently, undervaluing their imports and thus lowering their duty payments while overvaluing their exports and earning more foreign exchange credits than they deserve.[4] If nothing else, too much countertrade gives a country an inaccurate picture of its economy.

THE PRICE OF IMPORTS IS FORCED UPWARD

Not only does countertrade tie up a nation's export revenues, it raises the price of its imports as well. As the adage goes, "There's no free lunch," and third world nations are no exception. At first countertrading nations may do well. But once the large international businesses catch on—which doesn't take long—up go the prices to cover the countertrade costs.

Just because companies from the developed world are fiercely competitive does not mean this will not happen. MNCs can afford eventually to raise the price of their products to those countries mandating countertrade because countertrade demands increase the cost structure of all MNC competitors. Therefore, when the countertrade discount runs an average of 10 percent for every vendor trying to sell to a country mandating countertrade, it is no different than if respective material costs rose by roughly a proportional amount.

A VICIOUS CREDIT CIRCLE IS CREATED

Supposedly, countertrade helps third world countries strike better bargains and expand their net exports. This may change soon, however, because third world countries have unwittingly created something of value: the countertrade credit. By insisting that MNCs countertrade if they want to overcome trade restrictions, third world countries have created a new and lively business called the countertrade credit business. Essentially, for hefty fees the countertrade business does what the free trade system used to do at no cost. That countertrade is growing suggests that international trade is losing its efficiency and becoming harder to manage in an economical manner.

The impression third world countries give as to the way they would like to see international trade is that *only* third world countries could demand (or allow) the countertrade, and *only* their goods (the ones they can't sell for cash) could qualify for countertrade.

Many government officials in the Third World believe that their cash goods, the proceeds of which they use for interest payments and the purchase of high-priority items, are off-limits to countertrade. Previously, sales and purchases in and out of a country were two independent transactions, as shown in Figure 4-2. The host country could use the cash it earned any way it wished.

Several years ago, third world nations began toying with countertrade when their disposable net foreign earnings declined. By demanding—or permitting—countertrade as a means of selling their slower moving products, third world countries learned that countertrade was beneficial. Figure 4-3 shows how this was done.

What third world countries did not anticipate was that MNCs would demand countertrade, too. Even now, companies that purchase large quantities of goods from the Third World are demanding that countertrade credits be included in the deals. These companies will pay cash just as before. Only now they are insisting the cash they pay be earmarked to pay for products the host government may not necessarily want, as is shown in Figure 4-4.

Some MNCs use the credits they receive for their own future sales into the host country. Others sell the credits—for as much as 15 percent of their stated value—to other MNCs that use them to sell their own products into the host country. Trading companies like UNIVEX

Figure 4-2.

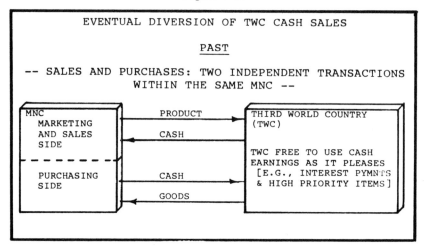

Figure 4-3.

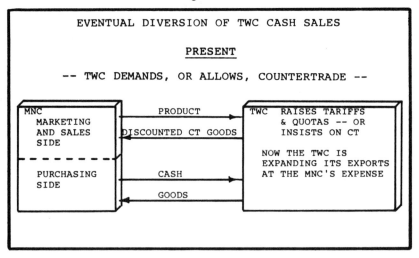

Figure 4-4.

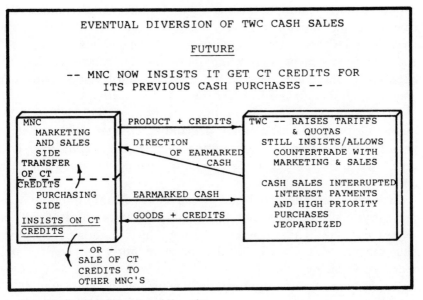

EVENTUAL DIVERSION OF TWC CASH SALES

FUTURE

-- MNC NOW INSISTS IT GET CT CREDITS FOR
ITS PREVIOUS CASH PURCHASES --

and banks like the First Boston have already investigated ways to facilitate the trading and sale of countertrade credits.

When the MNC plays the countertrade game, some of the cash earnings of the host country are tied up for uncertain and uncontrolled use. There is no doubt about it: Countertrade is financial hostage-holding which can be done on both sides. The result is an increasing restriction on both the MNC's and the host country's cash earnings. Certainly, the host country can refuse to give countertrade credits. But now they are in the same position as MNCs trying to sell to them: they must either grant the credits or lose the sale.

With the dollar strong, third world goods have been more competitive. But now that the dollar is dropping, the trading strength of the Third World may decline, and countertrade may backfire. As Figure 4-4 implies, a third world government can refuse to grant credits when it sells its own goods to the developed world. But it has to have a strong negotiating position to do this. If not, its only alternative to granting credits is to limit countertrade with MNCs. In so doing, it dries up the secondary market for its credits and makes it unprofitable for buyers to sell them.

However, the situation could go in the opposite direction, with countertrade becoming a vicious circle. If third world country A is having trouble moving its goods, and if competing third world countries B and C are granting credits to sell their goods, third world country A may elect to give out more credits in order to keep its exports moving. However, the more credits third world country A grants, the less control it has over the use of its earnings.

At present, the trend is in this direction, which explains why many third world countries are demanding countertrade for higher priority items: They are attempting to steer the credits they give out toward the purchase of items they would purchase for cash anyway.

In both cases, the end result is the same. Countertrade, as it is presently practiced may not appreciably increase third world net export earnings. Thus countertrade may fail in its original purpose, becoming instead a commercial hydra that hurts the Third World more than it helps it.

While in the South countertrade is mandated by governments, in the North countertrade could be mandated by large-scale purchasers. As an example consider the following hypothetical scenario:

Imagine yourself seated in Mr. Byer's office discussing the pros and cons of countertrade. Mr. Byer is a purchasing agent for Multinational Inc., a bluechip company. Suddenly, the phone rings. It is the sales agent from one of Mr. Byer's suppliers in a third world country. As Mr. Byer motions you to stay seated, you remain and listen to his end of the conversation.

"Hello? Oh, hello, my good friend, Juan Ramirez. I am delighted to hear from you again. How are you?

"Ha, ha, ha. That's so nice. Everything here is going very well, too. Except for the weather. It is very cold. I wish I were in your wonderful city with you, enjoying the sunshine.

"Yes?

"That's okay.

"Yes. Ahhb, I'm not sure.

"No, not yet.

"Ahhb, . . . I don't know if I can give you that order we discussed several months ago.

"Well, . . . it's a long story. You see, our corporate strategy has been changed toward diversifying worldwide purchasing of everything our company orders. I'm sure you understand . . . fluctuating exchange rates, shipping costs, price differentials, political instability, things like that.

"What?

"Oh, Juan, please don't get that impression. I know we negotiated the price. But price isn't the primary thing at issue in this instance. I have these other considerations to think about now, that's all. And regardless how either of us feels, policy is policy at corporate headquarters, and there's nothing either of us can do about it, is there?

"Yes.

"Yes.

"A-hum, . . . a-hum.

"Now, let's keep calm, Juan. I think I will be able to give you the order anyway. But before we go on, there is one small matter I need to discuss with you. It's only a formality and it will only take a minute.

"That's right.

"Ahh, . . . what are you and your government prepared to take in countertrade in the event I cut you a purchase order for those whizzits you want to sell us?

[Long pause]

"Juan? . . . Are you still there?

"Countertrade, Juan.

"It's spelled *c-o-u-n-t-e-r-t-r-a-d-e.*

"It's a kind of barter. . . . international barter.

"Yes. That's right. You understand now.

"We want you to take something in return from us instead of cash. Then, you sell it in your domestic market—or in another country—and keep the proceeds as your sales revenues.

"That's right! Actually, everything is quite straightforward here. No government to mess with . . .

"Right!

"I am sending you a complete packet of everything our company sells given me by our marketing department. You can chose anything you like inside this seventy-eight-page catalog up to, or beyond, the amount of our order from you. In particular, I am dog-earing pages 34 and 47, which might be of real interest to you.

"Yes.

"Yes.

"I am perfectly aware that my company has been a regular cash customer of yours for the last three decades. But times have changed, Juan. If you remember, two years ago your government banned a number of my company's products and levied stiff import license restrictions and tariffs on all the rest. And when my company sells products into your country we often have to countertrade. So, what's fair's fair, and why shouldn't you countertrade with us?

"Yes.

"Yes.

"That's a good point. We understand that your government is short on foreign exchange right now. We also know that it looks at our products as, how do you call it, 'non-essential items?'

"But we have to make a living, too. Just like everyone else, we either make a profit or we go out of business. Even so, we did one more thing. We know your government likes armaments. So we contracted with several arms manufacturers in our country who would be willing to sell you arms. Aah, . . . I'll be selling them the countertrade credits you'll be giving me.

"What's that?

"An impossible burden for your company?

"Come on, Juan. Buck up! You can do it! I know you can. Why, my company has been doing it for the last several years now.

"I beg your pardon?

"I might have to do without because you're afraid you might not be able to make me the sale?

"Awh. . . . I'm sorry to hear that. But you know, everybody is selling whizzits these days. Why, I was reading a report just yesterday which said that over a dozen third world and socialist countries are fighting for the international whizzit market. And I swear that I must have gotten at least a half dozen calls in the last two weeks from third world competitors trying to do business.

"Well, Juan, you know what they say in the countertrade business: 'You either countertrade, or you don't make the sale,' ha, ha.

"I'm sure you might want to take a day or two to think about these things. But as I said before, they're just a formality we're applying now to everybody. So as soon as the first supplier agrees to countertrade, all other things being equal, we'll award them our purchase contract.

"I hope yours will be one of the more aggressive companies to countertrade with us, Juan. I did enjoy buying whizzits from you all these years, really I did. We've had some real good times together. I'd like to continue our relationship.

"Yes.

"Yes.

"Good bye, Juan."

Mr. Byer puts down the phone and resumes his discussion with you about countertrade.

PROTECTIONISM IS ACCELERATED

Countertrade could turn out to be a major source of contention between developed countries and the Third World. As it continues to expand, resistance against it is building up in the developed world. The U.S. and British governments; the Western European governments; and the IMF, GATT, and the World Bank claim that countertrade will eventually reduce world trade. Even the United Nations Conference on Trade and Development (UNCTAD) predicts that the balance of payments situation in third world countries will not improve and bilateralism will grow. Although UNCTAD supports countertrade between private businesses, especially in the case of South-South trade, it disapproves of government-to-government bilateralism.[5]

Traditionally Japan and Europe's protectionist barriers have exceeded those of the United States. But Americans feel threatened by what they see as unfair international competition. The trade deficit is worrisome. They believe other nations are taking a free ride on their efforts to maintain a free trade system by making as many export sales for cash as they can, while requiring those who want to sell to them to countertrade.

Complaints of lost sales are increasing in the United States. Between 1980 and 1984, sixty-nine companies responding to a U.S. International Trade Commission survey indicated they had lost about $1.0 billion worth of deals because of countertrade requirements.[6] A turning point for countertrade will occur when the United States finally says, "We don't have any foreign exchange either, so we're mandating countertrade, too."

Countertrade is stirring some bad blood. Dumping charges are being lodged, with countertrade cited as one of the culprits. As countertrade demands increase, some exporters will stop selling their products into the international marketplace.

A number of companies refuse to enter countertrade deals because they fear that once they start in a country they will have to continue indefinitely. Therefore, some managers prefer to sell elsewhere for cash rather than get involved with complicated transactions with host governments.

In addition, the developed world is becoming increasingly protective of its high technology. Nations view technology as their marketing edge, and there is growing concern that today's recipients of technology transfer will be tomorrow's competition. Companies are even more sensitive to this issue than governments, as they know best what their technology is worth.

The Seat deal was a prime example of this. A number of years ago, Fiat decided to set up an auto assembly plant in Spain. Several years later, Fiat withdrew. The Spanish government took over the plant, evidently pumped in some capital, and started producing Seat's, a Fiat look-alike, which were sold all over Spain and then exported in other Mediterranean countries.[7]

MONEY IS HELD HOSTAGE

Buybacks occur when a developed world company sends a turnkey plant to a third world country. The third world country then pays for the plant in output over a number of years. Critics of buyback deals contend that while the plant supplies the product to the host country itself, the goods given in payment increase competition in the international marketplace.[8]

Western firms have little control over the delivery and quality of goods taken in payment from Eastern Europe and the USSR. It can be a long time before investing firms receive their first shipment from the plant. Often, the waiting period is extended by slow construction, and technical, training, and, political problems in the host country. The longer the length of the transaction, the easier it is for substitution of goods, other than the ones originally agreed upon, to take place. As time goes on, the host country may decide it can sell for cash items it has already included on the countertrade list. Thus, it looks for ways it can restrict those goods.[9]

If commodity prices swing in either direction, buybacks can cost the receiving company money. If prices fall, investors may pay a higher price for items they could buy for less. If prices rise, the exporting company may refuse to sell them.

Occidental Petroleum sent a turnkey ammonia plant and phosphate fertilizers to the Soviets in exchange for the ammonia produced. But even Occidental's Armand Hammer can't call them all right. Occidental's problem had to do with the amount of time (fifteen years) it will take to complete the deal, which was begun several years ago. Since that time, Occidental has been squeezed from two directions: not only did the market price of ammonia fall, but the cost of producing phosphate went up.[10] Supposedly, hedging answers the dilemma of commodity price fluctuations, but hedging extends only so far into the future and is extremely expensive.

Oil barter also could cause major headaches in this respect. As long as oil prices are falling, oil barter may serve a purpose. But once a country or company signs a barter deal with an oil producing country, if the price of oil goes up those receiving the oil might find themselves waiting a long time.

Because the MNC may not be paid for a number of years, it can be held hostage by the third world country until the transfer of managerial and technical expertise is complete. In addition, the possibility of political vulnerability increases with deals that extend over a long period of time.[11] Much of the concern over the Soviet pipeline deal stemmed from administration fears that Western Europe would become dependent on natural gas from the USSR.

In governments and industry alike in the developed world there is increasing objection to unfair competition from countertraded goods. Affected unions don't like it. Companies are hurt, and workers are displaced because of countertraded imports competitive with their own products, but undersold by the subsidy often inherent in a countertrade deal.

The U.S. textile industry believes that mandated countertrade forces companies wishing to sell their products into a country to take back textiles, subsidize them, and make sales that otherwise would not have taken place. Similarly, the U.S. tourist industry has objected to using tour packages in countertrade offsets. It believes it is effectively taxed twice when it pays to support the defense industry and then loses business when tour packages are taken in payment. Such tour packages must favor foreign air carriers and foreign hotel chains in order to generate the maximum use of offset credits.[12]

If the developed world tries to curtail countertrade, third world countries will doubt its sincerity as long as countertrade continues to exist in the developed world's own back yard. According to an International Trade Commission study, in the five years between 1980 and 1984, some 70 percent of all counterpurchases done by American companies involved military offsets. A $500 million deal between Northrop and Switzerland involved the sale of 72 F-5s in exchange for Swiss products.[13] What is more, almost half American companies' countertrade was done with NATO countries, and only a small percent with Latin America.[14]

Countertrade offsets involving military procurement have become so common they are almost expected by countries purchasing arms. According to offset experts O'Sullivan and El-Abd, arms purchasers impose offset requirements to increase their own exports. In recent years, military offset demands around the world have skyrocketed to the point where the majority of them equal or exceed 100 percent.[15]

McDonnell-Douglas's sale of $2.4 billion F-18 jets to Canada illustrates how desperate the situation has become. The agreement required McDonnell-Douglas to give Canada $2.9 billion worth of benefits for the next decade and a half; this included a $350 million parts contract with Canadian firms.[16] However it wasn't long before the Canadians got their comeuppance. In the summer of 1984, when Belgium purchased 2,500 Land Rovers from Bombardier of Canada, the Canadians had to swallow an offset fully three times greater than the price of the vehicles simply to keep Mercedes in Germany from making the sale instead.

In many military sales transactions, both direct and indirect offsets are used. In order to maintain control over the technology and production, U.S. corporations are increasingly using indirect offsets. As a result, many U.S. arms builders have acquired hefty offset commitments.[17] But if the offset is indirect, other U.S. industries may be hurt due to an increased flow of other goods coming back to the United States.

McDonnell–Douglas, alone, has over $7 billion in offsets to be moved within the next ten years, and it is by no means alone. One question becomes whether or not American industry is taking on an undeclared debt, a debt not recorded in U.S. balance of payments records.[18]

Even when labor rates are low, short production runs can increase the cost of direct offsets. Set-up and training costs may drive the end cost of the parts above what it would cost were the same parts produced in the United States because the production run is too short to make the unit cost competitive. However, some host countries are willing to overlook this if they feel that the gains of technology transfer and increased employment offset increased costs.[19]

WORLD TRADE IS REDUCED

For the past few years the trend has been away from multilateral trade toward bilateralism. Increasingly countertrade is being used to balance bilateral accounts. While countertrade retards trade imbalances, it does so at a price. For instance, Malaysia used to buy its rice from Thailand (with which it was in debt) rather than from Burma (with which it had a trade surplus). Malaysia switched its purchases of rice from Thailand to Burma in an effort to better balance its two bilateral accounts. From a foreign exchange standpoint, the problem was alleviated.[20]

But what about the Thai rice growers? They may grow better rice, more cheaply and more efficiently, and with better service and delivery than the Burmese rice growers. And what about the Malaysian consumers? They pay more. So Burma wins, and Thailand and the Malaysian consumers lose.

How are Thai rice producers supposed to compete in the world marketplace if traditional purchasers suddenly stop buying for reasons completely out of the Thai's control? How does this affect Thai rice planners? Malaysian consumers? How is market stability increased if governments arbitrarily intervene in this fashion?

In fact, a country can use countertrade in its clearing transactions as a method for forcing other countries to subsidize its export sector. For example, all a country like Burma would have to do would be to establish a number of bilateral trade agreements with other third world nations and then import more from them than it exports. As Malaysia's partners became more pressed to clear the accounts, they would become more willing to take marginal, overpriced Burmese exports and thus finance Burma's export sector. At the same time, Burma would have the equivalent of interest free loans for as long as its foreign exchange debts were outstanding.

Historically, bilateral trade has led to wars and imperialism. Part of the reason Japan attacked Pearl Harbor was because the United States, its primary source of oil, had cut supplies off because of Japan's Manchurian campaign. Unwilling to give in to American demands, the only way Japan had to get oil in a non-free trade world was to bypass Singapore and the Philippines to the oil fields in Java. In large part, the war in the Pacific was fought over resources in a bilaterally trading world. Bretton Woods and free trade were intended to dispense with that.

Barter and countertrade do not allow companies and countries to sell or buy where they wish. This causes international trade snits which can grow into serious confrontations. Zimbabwe, for example, had a dispute with India not too long ago, over an agreement to take $1 million worth of Indian mining equipment in exchange for some $3.9 million of Zimbabwean asbestos. After the Indians had taken the asbestos, the Zimbabwean mining company decided to spend the $1 million cash to purchase U.S. mining equipment because it felt it was better than the Indian equipment.[21] In this instance, countertrade resistance occurred in a totally third world environment and because certain parties were not satisfied with the products they had agreed to have shipped.

Countertrade and bilateralism inject rigidity into the international trade system. Bilateral trade tends to lock countries into specific trading relationships, making it more difficult to respond to changing conditions and eventually increasing imbalances.[22]

With bilateralism, the trade between two countries can go no further than the exports of the weakest partner. In addition, requiring each set of accounts to be balanced individually reduces trade, whereas accounts opened through multilateral clearing systems does the opposite.[23]

Countertrade perpetuates inefficiencies. It encourages the production of excess goods by locking parties into what often becomes Byzantine deals. Transactions are not decided on competitive grounds. Countertrade introduces government intervention and bureaucratic allocation in the marketplace when it has been shown repeatedly that government involvement reduces the volume of total trade in a free trade system. And, like government programs, once institutionalized, countertrade may continue long after it has outlived its usefulness. Some economists look upon countertrade as the international kudzu of the 1980s: a vine that if left unattended will choke free trade. The problem is that it is almost impossible for companies and governments to avoid countertrading unless everyone stops at once.

SPECIAL PROBLEMS

The Craft Industry

Handicrafts, as the name implies, are those items made by hand or with simple machines. Usually, the subject comes up in discussions of countertrade with the Third World. Ostensibly, crafts should provide a good starting point as many third world countries already have expertise in the area. Yet MNCs turn away from crafts primarily because they don't know how to overcome the constraints.

The craft industry in many third world countries is presently at a rudimentary stage. Even though some craft businesses are selling for cash, their marketing activity is almost nonexistent. Many have no catalogs or brochures. They simply wait for the customer to come to them. Willing customers in the developed world often have little idea what is available. Unable to maximize the marketing potential of their goods, the third world craft industry winds up underpricing its products. Consequently, they have slim margins and operate on shoestring budgets.

But there are other constraints germane to the craft industry as a whole. Customers require a limited number of crafts: a few of them go a long way. Additionally, almost all nationalities make crafts. Thus, the competition is fierce.

What sells crafts?

- Utility
- Novelty
- Beauty
- Quality
- Quantity
- Availability
- Marketing
- And the right price

Many third world crafts don't do well against these standards. (Many developed world crafts don't either.) One obvious problem is quality. Many third world crafts are not of the quality the developed world wants. For one thing, most are made by hand rather than machine, thus making it impossible to stamp out thousands of better units. But increasing quality takes time because it requires raising the skill level of workers.

Third world craftsmakers are far away from their developed world markets. Whereas craftsmakers in the developed world can stroll through gift shops and department stores to get a sense of what sells, most craftsmakers in the Third World have never seen the inside of a department store. Thus, they are at a disadvantage determining which styles sell well and which do not.

Crafts that sell well to tourists inside the host country may not do as well abroad. Craftsmakers within the host country are better able to ask customers what they like. Tourists, on the other hand, often buy crafts primarily as a remembrance of their visits.

The third world craft industry is partially blinded by circumstance. Helping third world craftsmakers see the market more clearly would offer a partial solution to their difficulties, a service that many MNCs are admirably suited to provide. The challenge for a profit-making company in the third world crafts industry is not to train people who know nothing about crafts, but to assemble the best native craftsmakers and train them to make their crafts of such quality that prices—and margins—will be raised.

Pat Ballard, of the Cheney Group, did just this type of thing when she searched Jamaica for local art. She found an excellent Jamaican artist with works located in a number of local museums and selected several of his best works to be mass produced and sold through a distribution network in the United States. Said Ms. Ballard, "It was very good countertrade—we made money, the client made money, and the artist made money—which is one of the prime criterion of my doing countertrade. If it isn't beneficial all around, I won't do it." The deal is expected to continue on an ongoing basis.[24]

The incremental increase in craft revenues could be used to get countertrade credits. One way to countertrade crafts is simply to help people to improve the quality and increase the volume of what they are already making. An outstanding example of a third world craft industry getting on its feet is Things Jamaican, located in Kingston. This government-sponsored company for profit was revived by the Seaga Administration after languishing for almost a decade. Things Jamaican makes over a thousand items, many on its premises, that cover the spectrum of the craft industry. The rest of its products are made by Jamaicans working in their own homes and villages. Things Jamaican helps train these people and acts as a cooperative and clearing house for their goods. Thus, it allows the craftspeople to remain in their homes and concentrate on their craft skills while relieving them of the marketing and distribution function. By applying modern business practices to a traditional industry, Things Jamaican has experienced remarkable growth. Thus, this company can serve as a model for MNCs wishing to establish similar operations in other countries.

Small Country Competition

Small third world countries have their own special problems. The small Caribbean island nations come to mind, but any small country will do. Some MNCs are reluctant to engage in countertrade agreements with such countries as their markets are too small to warrant the costs involved in beginning export trade. One solution to this problem is that the MNC could generate excess credits over what it sells into such a country and then sell these credits on the open market in the United States for cash. Proceeds collected from the sale of the credits (probably between 5 percent and 10 percent of the value of the credits) to other corporations also needing entry to this host country would then help cover the costs incurred by MNC. Because in this situation the MNC's market is small, its investment will be relatively small as well as its downside risk. With a small downside risk, the MNC can afford to experiment with different ways of starting up small entrepreneurial ventures in third world countries until it gains expertise and finds a generally applicable formula for success. Using this prototype the MNC could set up a creative countertrade operation in excess of its needs, get the credits, send in the product, and re-export what it could not sell to other soft currency countries.[25]

Small countries need to have close enough economic ties with one another so that they can offer the MNC a market large enough to warrant the time and effort expended to set up creative countertrade operations. Otherwise, the benefits of this concept will be skewed toward those third world countries with larger domestic markets.

The Information Deficit

One of the problems confronting both the MNCs and the third world countries is an information deficit. People are not getting the information nor the exposure to conditions in other parts of the world required to evaluate opportunities properly. Greater effort must be made by both groups to anticipate, understand, and appreciate the needs of the other better.

MNCs can easily obtain information about foreign countries. Understanding what the information means is more difficult. The flow of information, understanding, and appreciation between North and South is inadequate. Because of this, both sides miss numerous opportunities. And the international arena is the one with the greatest opportunity.

More first-hand information of the type gleaned from conferences and travel is needed. The Caribbean Basin Investment Exposition and the Miami Conference on the Caribbean, conferences held back-to-back in Miami every December, offer a superb way of meeting these needs.

Top government and business leaders from twenty-six Caribbean Basin countries attend the conferences and exchange views with their counterparts in the United States and Canada on a wide range of topics. Not only does each country present an orientation and overview of its national business opportunities, each also provides display exhibits, one-on-one appointments in country business suites, and relevant informational literature. Speeches are given at lunches and dinners by the highest-ranking members of business and government of both regions.

Expositions of this sort offer executives the chance to speak with a large number of influential people ready to consider new business opportunities and ideas, and this with a relatively small outlay of time and expense. The U.S. government will actually finance business tours to foreign countries under certain circumstances.

Numerous experiments are being made with countertrade to find out what works and what does not. Although it has many facets, countertrade is no different than any other new phenomenon in that it will soon mature and settle into its niche in the scheme of international trade.

Our conclusion is that countertrade is a limited-use trade vehicle. Within its constraints, which we call creative countertrade, it can do an admirable job overcoming foreign exchange problems and helping MNCs and third world countries work together. It is a superb catalyst for this kind of development.

But no form of countertrade is a substitute for free trade. The over use of it in this manner will only get in the way of better ways of doing business and will slow down trade by entangling it in complications. We believe countertrade—important as it is—will never be a major part of world trade. It cannot be. It will remain on the periphery of free trade, ebbing and flowing over the years as conditions warrant.

NOTES

1. Secretariat, "Countertrade: Developing Country Practices," Organization for Economic Cooperation and Development, Paris, 1985, p. 25.
2. *Countertrade Outlook*, December 17, 1984, p. 2.
3. *Countertrade Outlook*, December 16, 1985, p. 2.
4. "Countertrade: Developing Country Practices," p. 25.
5. *Countertrade Outlook*, January 27, 1986, p. 1.
6. *Countertrade Outlook*, November 11, 1985, p. 2.

7. Jane Rippateau, "Countertrade Activities in the Auto Industry, Part I Europe," *Countertrade and Barter Quarterly* (Spring 1985): 41–43.

8. "Growing Worries over Buyback Deals," *Chemical Week*, June 2, 1982, pp. 36–43.

9. "Growing Worries."

10. "New Restrictions on World Trade," *Business Week*, July 19, 1982, pp. 118–22.

11. Peter C. Beutel, "The Changing Relationship of Energy and Countertrade," Countertrade Seminar, World Trade Center, New York, N.Y., December 16–17, 1985.

12. *Countertrade Outlook*, June 24, 1986, p. 1.

13. Everett G. Martin and Thomas E. Ricks, "Countertrading Grows and Cash Short Nations Seek Marketing Help," *Wall Street Journal*, March 13, 1985, p. 1.

14. "Data on Countertrade Issued by International Trade Panel," *American Metal Market*, November 6, 1985, p. 16.

15. Hesham El-Abd and Michael O'Sullivan, "U.S. Military Offsets—Net Benefits or Costs?" *Countertrade and Barter Quarterly* (Autumn 1984): 50–52.

16. Philip Maher, "The Countertrade Boom: A Crummy Way to Do Business. . . . But Here's How to Do It," *Business Marketing*, January 1984, pp. 50–56; David Hurst, "Government Turns a Blind Eye as British Countertrading Blossoms," *Countertrade and Barter Quarterly* (Autumn 1984): 53–57.

17. El-Abd and O'Sullivan, "U.S. Military Offsets."

18. Ibid.

19. Steven Graubart, "Offsets: Past and Future," *Countertrade and Barter Quarterly* (Autumn 1984): 58–59.

20. John L. Griffin and J. Rand William Rouse, "Countertrade as a Third World Strategy of Development," *Third World Quarterly* (January 1986): 177–204.

21. *Countertrade Outlook*, November 25, 1985, p. 3.

22. "New Restrictions on World Trade."

23. "Countertrade, Developing Country Practices."

24. *Countertrade Outlook*, January 7, 1985, p. 2.

25. Audley Shaw, interview with author, Jamaica National Investment Promotion Ltd. headquarters, New York, N.Y., September 4, 1984.

5 CREATIVE COUNTERTRADE

This chapter and the one that follows examine a new form of countertrade—called creative countertrade.[1] To a great extent creative countertrade is an enhancement of the traditional forms of countertrade outlined in earlier chapters. Creative countertrade is a product of world economic and social changes. Finally, and most importantly, it provides methods for avoiding some of traditional countertrade's constraints.

MAJOR WORLD CHANGES

Social adjustments and economic realignments taking place throughout the world will have a major impact on the future form of countertrade. Until well into the next century the political, social, and economic relationship between the North and the South[2] will dominate international trade.

Peter F. Drucker, America's leading management consultant, states that since the early 1970s three structural shifts have occurred in the international economy: (1) an uncoupling of the world's industrial and commodity economies, (2) an uncoupling of industrial output and blue collar employment, and (3) a partial uncoupling of world trade and capital transfer.[3] To his list we have added four trends:

(1) the mushrooming of third world productivity, (2) the expansion of South–South trade, (3) the increased importance of the third world economy to the Developed World and (4) the increased cooperation of third world governments with MNCs. All of these changes will have a major impact on future forms of countertrade.

The Uncoupling of Industrial and Commodity Economies

The health of the world's industrial economy (primarily in the North) is no longer directly linked to the world's commodity economy (primarily in the South). Whereas, in the past, the two economies went into boom and bust cycles together, today this is not the case. Tin, foodstuffs, copper, silver, and bauxite, to mention a few, have remained depressed in spite of growth in the world economy. Commodities have played a smaller role in the world industrial economy because the value of primary-products has dropped to a given unit of the finished product. In the United States industries such as mining, oil, basic manufacturing, and farming now employ only 20 percent of the nation's workers, as opposed to 40 percent in the middle 1950s.[4] In the middle 1980s the economies of the North recovered nicely from the world recession, while commodity prices remained weak, leaving many third world nations in a cash flow bind.[5]

The uncoupling of the primary and finished product economies is causing third world countries to develop manufacturing exporting operations at breakneck speed. The South is turning away from its primary emphasis on the export of commodities toward a diversification of its industrial export base. For years small nations have felt vulnerable because of their dependence on one or two exports. But for many third world leaders the financial havoc caused by the plunge in commodity prices in the early 1980s drove home the point that action must be taken to diversify now.

A multitude of buyback countertrade deals have been established in an effort to diversify exports in foreign exchange poor countries. In recent years China has been a leader in this regard. Military offset transactions such as those between American aerospace manufacturers and Israel, likewise, represent an effort to diversify exports. The fact is that in the future the use of buyback transactions will increase, and additional new forms of countertrade will be explored.

The Uncoupling of Production and Employment

Output and employment in the industrial economy are no longer directly linked. In highly capitalized production, labor costs are being squeezed out of the finished cost equation. Blue collar labor is being replaced with knowledge labor and capital, which will, in turn, make it more difficult for third world countries to compete on wage rates alone.[6]

However, the world division of labor is still moving in favor of the nations of the South as they pick up managerial, technical, and marketing expertise from the North and from each other. In effect, there is a race taking place between the high-production, high-wage North and the comparatively low-production, low-wage South. While the North is automating (i.e., reducing direct labor costs) as fast as it can to remain competitive, the South is racing to raise the skill level of its cheap labor force. As is the case with Japan and the NICs, mechanization and skill levels have risen faster than wage rates. This has increased the price-productivity level and allowed them to set up fabrication and assembly facilities to make products no longer economically viable to make in the North. Although the labor advantage could swing back to the North sometime in the future, as Mr. Drucker maintains, especially as robotization becomes widespread it could be as long as a decade and a half before that happens across the board.[7]

For our purposes, the reduction of direct labor as a percentage of total cost will intensify third world efforts to create maximum technological and knowledge transfer. This, in turn, will necessitate the creation of new kinds of countertrade to accomplish the task.

The Partial Uncoupling of Trade and Capital Transfer

Trade is being surpassed by capital transfer as the primary mover in the world economy. Shifting exchange rates and movements in international credit are superseding the importance of the sale of products and services on the world stage.[8]

Because fluctuating exchange rates make it difficult to predict comparative labor costs, third world governments are more willing to participate in production-sharing agreements with MNCs, as such arrangements allow them to obtain labor-intensive assembly work in all but locked-in markets. Moreover, as it becomes easier to move capital, more creatively arrangements can be structured as a means of getting money invested in the Third World at acceptable risk levels. In this respect countertrade will play a key role.

The Mushrooming of Third World Productivity

Other trends are certain to influence the future of countertrade. Within the next two decades the information revolution will greatly increase third world productivity, transforming it into a world economic contender. The newly industrialized countries, described elsewhere in this book, are in the vanguard of this movement. Enhanced communication systems, expanding education, and increased interaction with other nations are already accelerating the flow of information and technology from the North to the South.

The Third World is leapfrogging over what was a long evolutionary period of development in the North, primarily because it can borrow from the North's learning and experience.[9] In a number of third world economic sectors the level of managerial and technological sophistication is growing. Witness growth in exports of steel from Mexico, shoes from Africa, textiles from Hong Kong, cars from Brazil, and video cassettes from South Korea. These are but a few examples of third world exports invading the markets of the Developed World.

Enhanced communication systems are already revolutionizing many third world countries. In 1983 NASA placed INSAT a new hundred million dollar telecommunications satellite above India, literally overnight. INSAT knitted the diverse and huge nation of India together through a television and telephone communications system that with conventional technologies would have taken billions of dollars and decades to accomplish. For the first time, villagers who formerly had had little or no contact with the outside were exposed to a new world of experiences and possibilities. Three American high-tech firms are planning a similar satellite system for China. Also, fiber optics technologies will both lower the installation cost of ground telecommunications systems and greatly increase their capacity.[10] Other regional systems are sure to follow.

One of the largest factors determining a nation's rate of development is the nature of its existing cultural values. For instance, the nations along the Western Pacific rim are moving most rapidly in the race to join the industrialized world in large part because their citizens have been able to adopt and internalize the values of industrial societies faster than some of their third world counterparts.

The nations of Africa and especially sub-Saharan Africa, on the other hand, beset with horrendous economic and social problems, are developing at a much slower pace. Latin America is progressing, but it has deep attitudinal problems, stemming from centuries of central control by a few families and the church, that hold it back. A number of the Moslem nations, which in a band from the Atlantic coast of North Africa east to Indonesia, are wrestling with the problem of assimilating technology with their religious and cultural values. Moslem frustration with the contradictory demands of new technology and their fundamental religious and cultural beliefs led to the Iranian revolution. In some respects it is easier to lash out at industrialized countries and their technological machines than it is to get in tune with a lifestyle that is both threatening and desirable.

But, traditional perceptions that have held people in check for centuries are rapidly giving way to more efficient and effective ways of doing things. One of the least appreciated but most potent results of the information revolution is technology's reduction of the unit (pupil) cost of education through attractively packaged, replicated, and disseminated information. Broadcast and video cassette television undoubtedly are the two most obvious examples. Not only do they entertain and teach at low cost, they also motivate people by exposing them to other, attractive lifestyles.

Raising the motivation level of nondeveloped societies, coupled with the transfer of information will induce nondeveloped nations to act to improve their lot on the grass-roots level. Higher motivation levels will translate into a more aggressive political posture, as can already be seen by the dominance of the third world nations in the United Nations, as well as some third world participation in international sporting events such as the Olympics and world soccer matches. Some of this increased motivation will have chauvinistic, extremist, and reactionary manifestations, as has been the case with the Red Guard in China and the major dislocations of societies like Iran, suddenly thrust from pre-industrial existences into twentieth-century technology. But much of it will be channeled into forging a

more competitive place for nondeveloped nations in world manufacturing and services.

Hundreds of thousands of students from the South are now studying engineering and science in the North as well as acculturating
themselves to northern societies. As they return home, they will
take new ideas with them and transfer their learning to others, and
thus expand the industrial and managerial class already present in
their home countries. Schools and universities are being formed or
expanded in poor nations where none existed before. Costa Rica, for
example, has several colleges that train engineers and managers.
These people will join that segment of the Costa Rican workforce
already at work transforming specific technologies into exporting
operations able to compete worldwide.

Third world economies will be impacted most by technology
because they have the furthest to go in terms of education, awareness, and economic development. Newly industrialized countries
(NICs), such as South Korea, Hong Kong, Singapore, Taiwan, Mexico, Brazil, and Argentina are examples of economies that have
grown at unprecedented rates in recent years. While some NICs may
stumble, most will continue to grow at twice the rate of the nations
of the North.

In any society, once the informational infrastructure takes shape,
new information can be pumped through at marginal costs per recip-
ient. Provided care is taken to convey information at the right pace
and with sensitivity to local norms, it will evoke a positive response
most of the time. At no time in human history will large parts of the
Third World be more receptive to new ideas and technology than in
the coming decades.

The Increase in South–South Trade

Greater South–South and South–Eastern bloc trade patterns are
emerging, indicating the development of trade relations among members of the Third World without participation from nations of the
developed world members. Much of this trade is being done on a
bilateral and countertrade basis. The Eastern European and South
American countries have established strong trade ties. Mexico and
Brazil are increasing their trade, and the nations of Africa are moving
increasingly toward regional trade. Third world leaders have known
for decades that much of their individual weaknesses vis-à-vis the

North could be offset by their members in political blocs. But third world countries are collaborating more than ever these days over a wider variety of things.

This trend is occurring because the world economy is simply getting larger. As local economies grow, it becomes far easier to do business with those close and familiar than with those far away and different. Historically, this trend is a significant event. It marks the first time third world nations have separated themselves from the demands and fortunes of the North. As they insulate themselves from economic fluctuations that in the past devastated them, they are pursuing healthier more independent foreign policies. Countertrade will increase as a result, because the Third World lacks the liquidity that free trade demands and because third world governments are more favorably disposed to countertrade than governments in the North.

An example of the trend toward increased South–South trade is the several billion dollars of foreign aid China gave to other third world countries in the 1960s, which in turn hastened China's shift away from communism in the 1970s. While the Red Guard was on the rampage in China, hundreds of thousands of Chinese were working on foreign aid projects in other third world countries. There, they both taught and learned from their hosts and brought back to China badly needed managerial and technological expertise.

A number of Caribbean and Latin American countries have sent delegations to Taiwan, Hong Kong, and elsewhere to expand trade and to get ideas on how they can increase growth in their own economies. Hong Kong has sent delegations to the Caribbean to see what could be done in the textile trade and the assembly of manufactured products under the tariff-free Caribbean Basin Initiative of the United States. Belize, worried about its sluggish economy and the threat of a Guatemalan invasion once the British Army leaves, even went so far as to offer Hong Kong businesspersons' citizenship and the equivalent of a $25,000 reward if they would immigrate there.

The Growing Importance of the Third World Economy

Third world markets have become much more important to developed world business than they were in the past, and they will continue to grow in importance.[11] As we have seen, this trend has been a major impetus behind MNCs' push to penetrate third world markets. But countertrade will continue to evolve in a manner that will allow both MNCs and the Third World to profit.

The Change in Attitudes in Third World Governments

Finally, third world governments, once hostile to MNCs, are now beginning to soften their approach and make investment easier. Many governments are chary about giving foreign business interests too much ownership and control over their resources and means of production, and with good reason. Some of this is changing. China is probably the best example. India, likewise, is becoming more business oriented, as are the Caribbean nations.

Increased contact between the Third World and other nations has been beneficial for all concerned. But events of the past have caused a number of third world nations to surround themselves with protective walls. MNCs trying to do business there can face more than bureaucratic red tape. They often face an active effort to limit their involvement. Many third world nations fear that if MNC activity is not held in check, local people will lose economic and political control. Moreover, MNCs may have to deal with societies that aren't so sure free enterprise is a good thing. It is not just Mr. Castro and Mr. Ortega who think free enterprise in the Third World equals exploitation.

What this means is that third world countries have limited their contact with other countries more than they might have done otherwise. In the process, they have limited their opportunities. In addition, they have adopted political and economic philosophies that often do not work well. Excessive centralization of decisionmaking, state ownership, and constraints on local companies' ownership and activities have held back many third world countries.

These perceptions, however, are being altered in favor of greater involvement with other nations and increased appreciation of the benefits of private enterprise. As a result, traditional barriers are coming down and new directions are being taken. Mexico had traditionally limited foreign ownership to 50 percent. Recently, it allowed IBM to build a plant there with 100 percent IBM ownership. China has opened its doors to outside investment. Jamaica used to be socialist. Now it has a governmental arm called JNIP (Jamaica National Investment Promotion, Ltd) that actively solicits private investment from inside the United States.

As the realization spreads that we all are dependent on citizens of other countries, collaboration becomes more possible. It is the inter-locking web of trade, finance, and capital in the world that will make people see the advantages of cooperation. As a result, MNCs will have an easier time overcoming resistance in third world countries. This shift will allow countertrade to take forms never before thought possible.

These trends will continue regardless of the fortunes of counter-trade, even though they will have a substantial impact upon it. Al-though all nations of the South will experience these trends, change will occur in some nations faster than in others. Generally speaking, the newly industrialized countries will develop the fastest, while some of the subSaharan African countries will have the most diffi-cult time. Moreover, change will occur within nations at different rates. Companies that produce high quality products for world con-sumption will exist next to abject poverty and will continue to do so for many years.

CHANGES IN TRADITIONAL COUNTERTRADE

Figure 5–1 depicts the spectrum of countertrade, with the least amount of involvement on the left and the greatest involvement on the right. Formerly, almost all countertrade was done on the left side of the spectrum with independent parties exchanging goods in spot trade deals. However, for the past decade, there has been a growing trend by MNCs to move to the right on the spectrum, due largely to the high cost and temporary nature of the left end. This trend began with the huge offset and coproduction deals hammered out in the 1970s between American arms manufacturers and the NATO countries and continued with numerous buyback deals with Eastern Europe, the USSR and China. Today there is a growing movement toward greater involvement (the right side of the spec-trum) with regard to third world trade.

Increasingly, third world countries are using countertrade as a development strategy. Leaders in those nations are taking a new look at their economic policies. Social development in the form of

Figure 5-1.

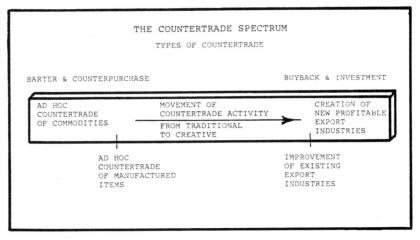

jobs, training, and technology transfer are becoming a major focus of countertrade arrangements.[12] Indonesia in 1982 instituted a policy that mandated countertrade for all imports over $500,000 for the express purpose of diversifying its exports and expanding its job sector. Colombia mandated countertrade several years later for similar reasons.

Corporations are being forced to take a more active role in these new types of ventures, as commodity traders are ill equipped to do so. The new types of countertrade are longer term, smaller in form at the beginning, and more evolutionary in nature.[13]

An example of this trend occurred about three years ago when General Motors was trying to get its trucks and automobiles into Jamaica. General Motors tried to get countertrade credits, but Jamaica had nothing to sell other than bauxite and handicrafts. Jamaica did have a low-cost, fairly well educated, and hard working labor force. Using a creative countertrade approach, Fred Tarter, president of Deerfield Communications and consultant to General Motors, leased an IBM computer and organized a typing pool to transcribe coupons, and survey questionnaire data and other forms of printed material shipped to Jamaica from the United States. What was exported out of Jamaica, then, were reels of magnetic tape and keypunched information to be used later in customer databases. The bugs were worked out while the Jamaican venture was still small. It is now a 300-worker, three-shift, seven-day-a-week operation in a free port zone in Montego Bay.[14]

Another example of this type of activity occurred in Eastern Europe. Dow Chemical recently developed parts for railroad cars for export from Romania where the production capacity to make them already existed. In turn, the Romanians took the products Dow wanted to sell there.[15]

Interaction Between MNCs and the Third World

As the two examples show, the major change taking place in MNCs business interactions with the Third World is that rather than simply trading manufactured items for commodities and some cash on an arm's-length basis, MNCs are finding themselves increasingly obliged to become highly involved—almost entwined—with their third world and socialist business partners.

Financing Third World Projects

While world trends are impacting countertrade, countertrade is impacting world trends as well. The United States and Western Europe are no longer capable of financing major development projects in the Third World. They no longer have the money. Too many developed world nations are in debt due to overspending. They can no longer afford to finance the needed foreign aid packages. Japan can provide some aid, but the OPEC countries can no longer do so. The international banking community is likewise overextended. This leaves private capital as the only major source of expandable financing left for the Third World, and the third world countries will try to use countertrade as a primary means of securing it.

Countertrade buyback techniques finance third world industrial expansion. In this instance, countertrade is a vehicle similar to supplier credit for small and start-up companies in the developed world: the MNCs, acting as the vendors for the Third World, supply the money and the expertise necessary for third world business to get up and running.

The Need for Something New

MNCs have three major governmental constraints limiting their sales of products in third world countries:

1. *Quotas*, which prevent products from entering the country
2. *Tariffs*, which raise the price of products so that few can afford to buy them
3. *Insistence* by the host government on countertrade in order for the MNC to make a sale. (As explained earlier, this is usually done on large construction or military contracts.) [16]

At the same time, third world countries have difficulty obtaining enough foreign investment capital to expand their net exports. Investment capital has three major sources, and each has its constraints.

Grant money is hard to come by and is not nearly enough to finance growth. *Loans* require good credit on the part of the host government and must be paid back with interest. *Private capital* provides a means for a third world country to obtain meaningful long-term financing. Competition is increasing among third world countries to obtain what limited amounts of private capital there are. Currently, private capital is not being invested in the Third World at a rate fast enough to expand net exports and relieve financial and social strains.

Traditional countertrade does not work very well, especially in terms of cutting through governmental restrictions for the MNC and increasing net exports for the host country. Coke got caught once with bathtubs from Eastern Europe and low-quality honey from China that fermented in a hot warehouse in Miami for two years. [17] In fact, traditional countertrade rarely addresses the tariff question at all, a major impediment to trade that hurts both the MNC and the host country. Consumer product companies, especially, face tariffs that drive up the street price of their products to several times what they would be in the developed world.

WHAT IS CREATIVE COUNTERTRADE?

Creative countertrade focuses on the capability of the host country's productive sector to create (and eventually produce) future goods (and services) for new market niches in the developed world and inside the MNC. Creative countertrade is stronger than business practices now in place because it attacks the problem in a more logical way: It looks to the *markets* first and the products second.

An aggressive and profitable creative countertrade operation not only allows the MNC to get more of its product into the country, it also allows it to sell more once it is there. In addition, it increases the host country's net exports. This is the essence of creative countertrade: it gives the MNC greater commercial leverage with the host government and the host government greater commercial leverage with the foreign investor.

Traditional countertrade focuses on existing goods to be brought out of the host country and sold in existing world markets. Thus, traditional countertrade must deal with the limitations of fitting what already exists into often unresponsive markets.

Creative countertrade, on the other hand, with its focus on creating future goods for new market niches has greater flexibility and wider possibilities. Creative countertrade is broader than countertrade. Not only does it include traditional countertrade, but also foreign investment and international joint venture activities. It carefully analyzes the needs of all the major parties and creatively applies existing business tools to answer these needs.

Traditional countertrade provides quick-fix solutions to ongoing trade problems. But it lacks the depth and longer time horizons of creative countertrade.

As can be seen in Figure 5-2, traditional countertrade has only one level of involvement. By contrast, creative countertrade can work in many ways. These levels range from traditional arrangements in which the MNC contracts with a local manufacturer to purchase a certain amount of unique or otherwise profitable goods year after year, to more complex alternatives that give the MNC a considerable degree of involvement, in terms of effort, time, and financial risk. Creative countertrade insists that the countertrade side of the transaction be at least a break-even operation for the MNC, whereas traditional countertrade does not. Traditional countertrade is usually a push-only proposition (Figure 5-3). The MNC's profit comes only from its own sales, with the countertrade side having to be subsidized.

Traditional countertrade presents difficulties because it attacks the problem of generating dollar payments in a backwards fashion. It looks to the goods to be sold first and to the markets in which they

Figure 5-2.

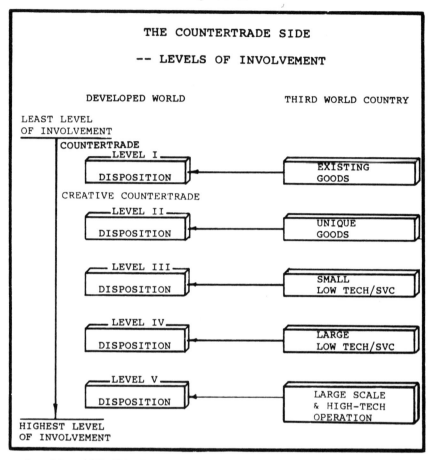

are to be sold, second. For example, General Motors sold 1400 Opels to Yugoslavia several years ago, and to its astonishment, was, with no prior notice, given a trainload of fresh strawberries in return. Although the strawberries were quickly sold, the GM manager handling the deal later described it as "awkward."[18]

Since goods that are marketed for cash are excluded from countertrade, the ones that are exchanged are often shabby, overpriced, or already picked over by other MNCs. Not surprisingly, the markets for such products are normally lukewarm. This is why a hefty discount must be paid to move the countertraded goods—a discount that comes right out of the MNC's revenues.

Figure 5-3.

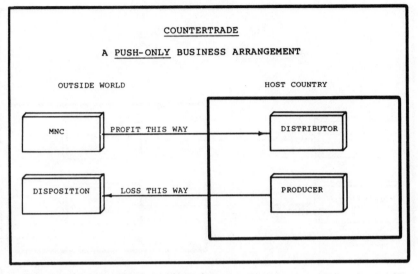

Because countertrade only partially addresses the needs of the host government, it lacks commercial leverage. Governments often negotiate countertrade deals with a take-it-or-leave-it attitude. Countertrade does not allow enough lead time for smooth operations and tends to be a one-shot affair. In addition, it requires large transactions in order to support administrative expenses.

By contrast, creative countertrade is a push-pull business arrangement (Figure 5-4). The countertrade side is at least a break-even proposition. Because profit is planned from the start, creative countertrade enhances the likelihood of profit on the return side. It is administratively cheaper because the costs can be spread over a longer period of time. In addition, it is more flexible because it affords a much greater latitude in terms of exchanged goods. Creative countertrade includes the goods that *can* be produced and is not limited to those that simply cannot be sold for cash.

Creative countertrade turns the traditionally weak countertrade leverage on its head. With traditional countertrade the buying country has the MNC over a barrel. In effect, the host country says, "Either countertrade with us, or we won't buy your product." In the end, the MNC usually has to pay to move the countertraded goods. Under creative countertrade everybody wins. Both sides are more

Figure 5-4.

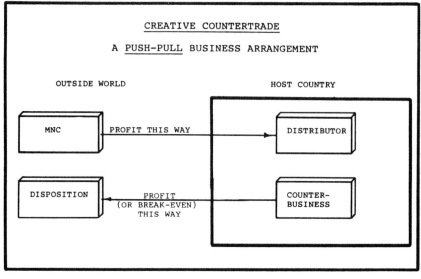

willing to do business because both stand to benefit from the arrangement.

The host country wants the MNC to increase its investment as this will increase the country's employment and exports. The MNC wants the host government to eliminate or reduce its quotas and tariffs on the MNC's products.

For example, in March of 1985 Boeing Aircraft won a $1.3 billion contract to lead a consortium of companies to build Saudi Arabia's Peace Shield air defense network. Boeing has a half billion dollar obligation to establish various high-tech and service industries in Saudi Arabia over the next ten years. The contract includes managerial and technological aid as well as the creation of production jobs. Among the industrial options considered were a $90 million plant making copper telephone wire, a $100 million facility producing telecommunications equipment, a $20 million data processing facility, aircraft repair facilities, a car part fabrication and assembly operation, and a computer software firm manufacturing Arab-friendly software for business and education.[19] In principal at least, all of these operations were capable of generating solid exports from Saudi Arabia.

Boeing is to ante $500 million. The venture is to be 51 percent Saudi owned, and some of the several hundred Saudi princes, each with his own oil allowance, will chip in another $500 million.[20] Although Saudi Arabia wanted all of its offset to be paid in high technology industries, after negotiating it agreed to have both service and manufacturing industries used in the offset.

HOW CREATIVE COUNTERTRADE WORKS

Creative countertrade recognizes that the MNC has investment capital that third world economies need. It also recognizes that it is the host government, in large measure, that prevents the MNC from selling more of its products in the host country's markets. Since the government is regarded as a customer and the MNC as an investment opportunity, each group will analyze the needs of the other—both real and perceived—and figure out methods, satisfying to both groups, for meeting those needs. When this happens the MNC will be more willing to invest in a third world economy, and the host government will be inclined to take down barriers in order to allow increased sales for the MNC.

The keys to a successful creative countertrade operation are that it is profitable and pays back start-up costs within a reasonable time. Figures 5–5 through 5–8 show how this is done.

Feasibility studies will give the MNC valuable information about the country with which it wants to do creative countertrade. The feasibility study, illustrated in Figure 5–5, examines potential market niches in the international community. In lieu of obvious market niches the MNC can see what a particular host country has that would fit the MNC's internal needs. At the same time, the MNC examines the host country's business sector to see if a business that could fill the MNC's need could be expanded or established there.

If a suitable possibility is discovered, the MNC drafts a tentative business plan for starting a business operation in the Third World. In the process, it may wish to talk to experts in similar businesses and make contact with potential entrepreneurs, suppliers, and distributors.

Finally, the MNC approaches the host government and says something like: "We are thinking about establishing a new export business

Figure 5-5.

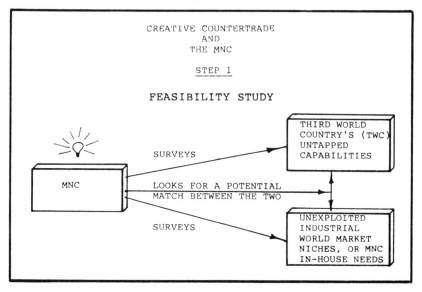

CREATIVE COUNTERTRADE
AND
THE MNC

STEP 1

FEASIBILITY STUDY

MNC

SURVEYS → THIRD WORLD COUNTRY'S (TWC) UNTAPPED CAPABILITIES

LOOKS FOR A POTENTIAL MATCH BETWEEN THE TWO

SURVEYS → UNEXPLOITED INDUSTRIAL WORLD MARKET NICHES, OR MNC IN-HOUSE NEEDS

in your country. This is the kind of business we are contemplating. Here are the advantages for your country. What kind of long-term foreign exchange credits and tariff benefits do you think your government might consider were we to set up this business and have it run successfully?"

If everything looks good, the business plan is implemented and the start-up phase begun (Figure 5-6). Here, the MNC uses its ideas, expertise, and investment capital either to establish a brand new business entity or to enlarge an existing one.

An example of such an arrangement is the agreement signed by the French restaurant, Maxims, to open a 600-seat restaurant in Peking, China. The restaurant could be regarded as a turnkey plant. Maxims, owned by Pierre Cardin, supplied the name, the interior art nouveau decor, one half the capital, and its culinary and business expertise. The Chinese, in addition to putting up their half of the needed capital, provided the labor, the day-to-day management, and most of the food and ingredients. The Chinese will buy back Maxim's equity as well as Maxim's share of the start-up costs over a ten-year period. Costs will be paid back at a predetermined profit level in hard currency generated from China's tourist trade.[21]

Figure 5-6.

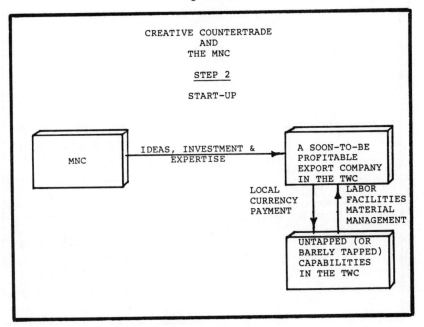

Note that the MNC is acting in its own interest, with profit making a priority. Likewise, for the Chinese profit-making incentives will streamline the process of getting the operation started.

In the third step, shown in Figure 5-7 the MNC actually brings the export operation into the host country and begins production. Here, the settling-in phase takes place, bugs are ironed out, and the MNC earns hard currency revenues. If need be, the MNC can provide distribution channels to move the export company's products, or it can buy them for its own in-house needs.

In the fourth step (Figure 5-8), the MNC enjoys the fruits of its labor and sells its (hopefully unencumbered) products in the host country's domestic markets. As its reward for setting up the operation, the MNC either shares in some of the profits or recoups its expenses, and receives countertrade credits and reduced tariffs for its own products.

The DeHavilland Aircraft Corporation of Canada is one of the companies zeroing in on creative countertrade. At a conference in

Figure 5-7.

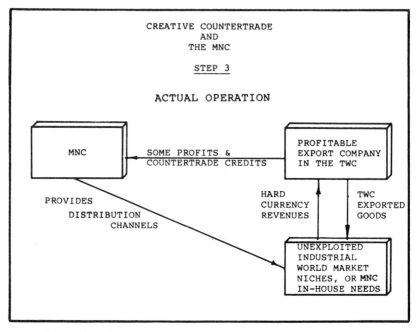

Figure 5-8.

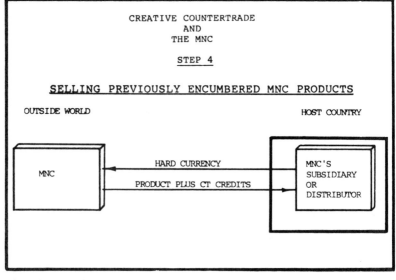

April of 1985, the director of that company's countertrade unit advised a strategy emphasizing the following points:

1. Get management ready early for an aggressive strategy
2. Go after the most profitable venture
3. Go for one program instead of several
4. Be certain the plan is attainable
5. Prepare to hold for the long-term
6. Realize the start-up may not bear fruit for a while
7. Keep the wording of the countertrade loose so that you don't get too restricted
8. Make sure that the new venture won't hurt your regular markets
9. Keep close to consultants, vendors, subcontractors, and marketers
10. Have inside personnel and at least one person in an office to coordinate the countertrade arrangement with outside parties; understand how the whole operation fits together.[22]

William Evonsky, of the General Electric Trading Corporation, is in favor of a creative countertrade approach in that he advises exploring the entire production and marketing potential of businesses in third world and socialist countries. He suggests finding a market with a good strong niche first, and then examining what can be done to create or upgrade a facility to make the market work.[23]

ADVANTAGES FOR THE UNITED STATES

The Multinational Company

Compared to its GNP, the United States exports a far lower percentage of its goods and services than do other developed countries. To overcome its trade deficit, U.S. business will have to establish new markets in India, China, Latin America, the Middle East, and other such areas within the next five to twenty years. Other potential markets are opening in Southeast Asia and Africa. Provided the U.S. government can develop a consistent foreign policy with a minimum of embargoes, Eastern Europe and the Soviet Union can be included as two large potential markets. Any method American business can find to penetrate these markets ahead of its international competitors will serve to increase U.S. exports and help alleviate the national trade deficit.[24]

MNCs use creative countertrade for a variety of reasons:

1. To gain a private source of foreign exchange so they can expand the market for their goods inside third world countries
2. So they can avail themselves of lower wage rates
3. So they can install the most competitive processing and plant technology
4. To get low-cost and often close sources of raw material
5. To assure gains in strong future markets.

Creative countertrade has the potential to increase the MNC's international sales by millions of dollars per year within several years. Longer-term, it could do more. With creative countertrade it is possible for the MNC to sell into any country, no matter how bankrupt, and even to negotiate selective tariff reductions (discussed later) in a number of countries around the world.

American Business

Some charge that creative countertrade competes with American business. They say that increased imports of cheap foreign-made products hurt American industry. There is no question that some segments of the American industrial base will be affected by an increase in creative countertrade. However, not all the goods coming out of the host country will be sold inside the United States. As noted earlier, only a fraction of the goods American companies take in countertrade ever make it to U.S. docks. Thus, the harm done is muted.[25]

On the U.S. export side, American industry is greatly aided. If the MNC is an American company, should its sales go up, its operations will expand and people will be hired. Moreover, increased exports from third world countries to the United States are already on the increase due to Japanese and the European export activity. U.S. industry is not going to escape the onslaught just because U.S. companies refuse to engage in creative countertrade. Thus, American companies might as well engage in creative countertrade and expand their export sectors as much as possible.

Banks

If it is done on a large scale, creative countertrade may aid international banks faced with loans to debtor nations. The crux of the international debt crisis can be summarized in one question: "What is the safest and most efficient way to transfer capital from North to South? By expanding alternative sources of capital, creative countertrade lifts sale responsibility for the financial burdens of the international debt crisis from the shoulders of the banking community.

The banking dilemma is well known: international banks are heavily exposed to countries that are practically bankrupt. Without more capital investment debtor nations cannot pay banks back. But if banks lend these countries more money, these nations will be even more heavily exposed than they are now and with little more assurance they will be able to recover. The banks are caught in a classic Chapter Eleven corner, only in this instance they cannot foreclose on the assets.

Contrary to popular belief, banks would be of limited use to third world countries even if they were not overextended. Vis-à-vis businesses in the Third World, banks are in the same position they are with start-up businesses at home. The character of the applicants is not always well established, the capacity of the business to repay the loan is yet to be determined, the collateral often will not cover the loan requested, and the conditions of the marketplace are often a guess. Third world businesses constitute too much risk for conservative establishments like banks.

Banks do not do well with start-up businesses because inevitably the payoffs on any one venture are never enough to cover the losses that are bound to occur on some of the others. Bad debts for bank loans are supposed to stay well under 3 percent. The same reasoning applies to bank loans to start-up businesses in the Third World. Banks are limited in their lending capacity because they must have assurance beforehand that the potential export company is a good credit risk.

As the only thing the banks can inject into the equation is financing, fledgling third world companies lacking the training, skills, or strength to qualify for a loan are excluded from the process. Thus, traditional bank financing can address only a fraction of third world countries' needs. Since that fraction represents the richest end of the economy, bank lending tends to perpetuate oligopolistic practices and lock out grass roots entrepreneurial growth.

Supporters of the traditional lending process will contend that government grants, subsidies, and guarantees can make up for these deficiencies. But today funding for these instruments has dried up. Even in the best of times much of the funding was misused as it was administered by government bureaucrats with little business knowledge and little direct control over fund expenditures.

Moreover, banks limit their lending to a certain percentage of value of the assets upon which they take a security interest. In start-up companies massive amounts of capital, often several times the value of the whole business, are needed. Knowing neither the business nor the technology intimately, lending officers are understandably cautious and conservative.

Through creative countertrade, the MNC is becoming the Third World's venture capitalist. But the payback comes not as much in the form of huge profits, as it does in the form of huge blocks of generated foreign exchange that the MNC can use to pay for the sale of its products into countries.

The MNC is in a better position than are the banks to see through difficulties and make the deal work. It sends in its own management, has more control over the operation, and has already figured out how to sell the output. MNCs with their entrepreneurial urge to get the export business rolling can serve as both a friend and a financier to third world countries.

The MNC investing in a buyback project for which it will be paid in products at a later date assumes a lower risk than a bank lending a traditional hard-currency loan to a third world company or government. The reason is due to the compartmentalization of the deal. The countertrade investor in comparison with a bank has a greater involvement in and understanding of how the money is being used. In many instances the countertrade investor has its own people participating on site in the project. This lowers the risk of (1) poor administration of the funds, (2) mismanagement, and (3) graft. It professionalizes the administration of the project by putting it in the hands of those people best trained and most motivated to manage it.

Second, once the government gives the go-ahead, it fairly much stays out of the managerial picture. Yes, the government may still meddle. But even when it does, the MNC has a major say in what is to be done, as compared with former times when the host government—or inexperienced local businessmen—had total control of overseeing the project.

Third, the MNC is not tied to the absence or presence of foreign exchange and is less affected by how the host country's economy is doing in general. Since equipment and expertise are the MNC's two primary inputs, and the physical product its return, this arrangement sidesteps most government and the banking red tape.

Fourth, creative countertrade gives the third world country a boost in that it relieves it of the burden of marketing and distributing the goods. Some might criticize this aspect of creative countertrade, claiming that it does not give the third world country an opportunity to develop a marketing and distribution network of its own. Yet all start-up ventures involve taking one step at a time. It is not uncommon, for example, for start-up companies in the United States to have other firms do not only their marketing and distribution, but also the entire manufacture of the product. Granted, the cost of doing this is high, and the company is not acquiring expertise it may need further down the road. But at the beginning, people can only do so much at a time, and it is more important to get the firm up and running, whether in the United States or in the Third World, than it is to force the company to do everything at once and ultimately fail.

One of the differences between countertrade financing and free trade financing is that with countertrade financing government guarantees are less required because the MNC has the equivalent of a security interest in the plant and equipment delivered. Additionally, there is strong goal congruence between the MNC, the host government, and the managers of the potential export company, as no one makes money until the deal works. Bank lending has never required this degree of solidarity. Once the bank made the loan the money could be stolen, wasted, or simply lost. Physical plants and equipment have the advantage of being more easily inventoried and less easily liquidated into cash.

While an increase in world liquidity will reduce traditional countertrade, as it did in the early 1970s, it is unlikely it will decrease creative countertrade as much. The Third World will voraciously import capital for at least the next 50 years. China at this time can still afford to make cash purchases because its international credit rating is still good. Yet China is doing more compensation and traditional countertrade deals than ever. Why? Because, regardless of the strength of the Chinese balance of trade, China still needs to import capital.

ADVANTAGES FOR THE HOST COUNTRY

Third world countries may benefit most from creative countertrade because it answers so many of their needs. Costa Ricans, according to a 1983 survey of that country, wanted the following:

1. Expand net exports—or at the least not using foreign exchange for "non-essential" items
2. Maximize capital flow into the country
3. Maximize transfer of technological and entrepreneurial know-how into the country
4. Increase employment, protect infant industries, and help local businesses share in profitable business opportunities
5. Keep foreign control of local industry to a minimum.[26]

Leaders of other Third World countries indicate they want pretty much the same things and have said so repeatedly in speeches, interviews, and articles. Creative countertrade meets many of their needs.

Net Exports

Creative countertrade is designed to expand the host country's net exports in order to generate the foreign exchange needed to sell the MNC's products into its markets. But more than that, it is intended to overcome the countertrade currency drain by generating at least as much foreign exchange as the host country expends on its purchase from the MNC.

Multinational companies often get into arguments with third world governments over the amount of the offset to be counter-traded. Beginning with a strategy to keep the offset as low as possible, they often set their limit at 100 percent. Most of the time MNCs trade at substantially lower levels. Ostensibly, a one-for-one swap is equitable. Corporate negotiators certainly think so: "Even-Steven," they say, "My stuff for your stuff; what's fair's fair," and so on.

Figure 5-9.

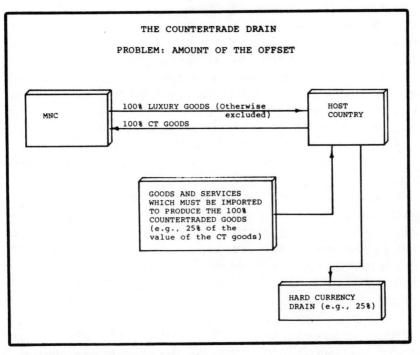

Yet a closer look reveals that a 100 percent offset may not be fair to the host government in terms of a zero foreign exchange loss that government must sustain. As Figure 5-9 shows, if the counter-traded goods require any kind of imports for their production, the amount of hard currency spent to acquire those imports constitutes a cash drain on the host country's balance of payments. On one small deal, it might not matter. But as a government policy, a large number of countertrade transactions like the one shown could damage the host country's financial health.[27]

There are several factors that could improve the situation, however. If hard currency has been invested to start up the export operation in the host country, it will tend to counterbalance some of the deleterious effects of the hard currency drain. If the export operation in the host country is brand new and appears to be permanent, and if the countertrade arrangement itself will last for only a number of years, the hard currency drain on the third world nation could be regarded as temporary and an investment in future cash export earnings. If either the export or the import operations are labor intensive and will result in many jobs, the training of workers can be seen as a means for raising the level of the host country's human capital, thus making it more competitive in other sectors.

So why do companies object so strenuously to more than a 100 percent offset? The diagram below tells why. In Figure 5-10 the discount is put at 10 percent, a not uncommon figure. In the first example in Figure 5-10, a 50 percent offset means that for every $100 of product sold, the MNC has to buy at least $50 worth of goods—which in this instance it can only sell for $45 (i.e., 10 percent off).

Because the percent discount pertains to the value of the goods being countertraded, the percent of the MNC's revenues on the discount costs depends upon the comparative values of the countertraded goods and the MNC's product (i.e. the offset). In other words, a fixed product base must support the discount. If the offset is less than 100 percent, the percent of revenues lost will be less than the percent of the discount. If it is over 100 percent, the reverse will be true.

Most companies pay to move the countertraded goods. They lose on the deal, especially when they go through a trading house or a bank. Because they pay a discount, which is a percentage of the *countertraded* goods, the value of the countertraded goods in comparison to the value of the product being shipped becomes critical in determining how much of a bite will be taken out of the company's revenues. The larger the offset, the larger the bite. That's why companies object to large offsets. But the host government wants the offset as high as possible in order to preserve foreign exchange.

So what do we have? We have the MNC and the host government at each other's throats: a game of hard-ball. Trust goes out the window. The MNC raises the prices of its products to cover its costs. The host government finds out about it and raises its tariffs. Each feels it is being hurt. Nobody's happy.

The problem is not who's right and who's wrong—they are *both* right, incidentally—the problem is two hungry parties fighting over too small a pie. The solution is to make a bigger pie, that is, make the countertrade operation profitable.

Contrast the discount problem with a positive offset leverage situation. As Figure 5-11 depicting positive offset leverage shows, pro-

Figure 5-10.

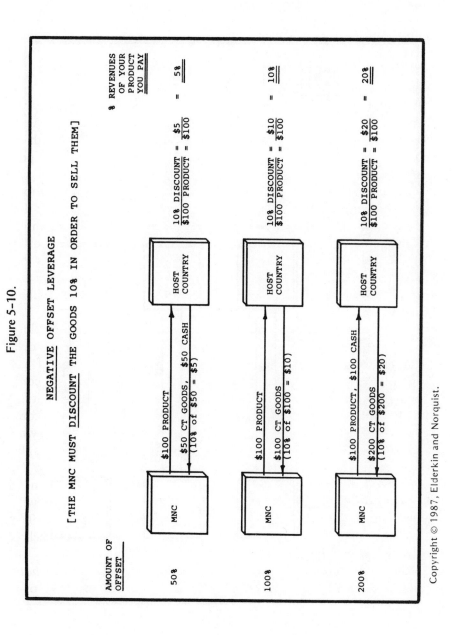

NEGATIVE OFFSET LEVERAGE

[THE MNC MUST DISCOUNT THE GOODS 10% IN ORDER TO SELL THEM]

AMOUNT OF OFFSET		% REVENUES OF YOUR PRODUCT YOU PAY
50%	MNC → HOST COUNTRY: $100 PRODUCT; $50 CT GOODS, $50 CASH (10% of $50 = $5)	$\frac{10\% \text{ DISCOUNT} = \$5}{\$100 \text{ PRODUCT} = \$100}$ = 5%
100%	MNC → HOST COUNTRY: $100 PRODUCT; $100 CT GOODS (10% of $100 = $10)	$\frac{10\% \text{ DISCOUNT} = \$10}{\$100 \text{ PRODUCT} = \$100}$ = 10%
200%	MNC → HOST COUNTRY: $100 PRODUCT, $100 CASH; $200 CT GOODS (10% of $200 = $20)	$\frac{10\% \text{ DISCOUNT} = \$20}{\$100 \text{ PRODUCT} = \$100}$ = 20%

Figure 5-11.

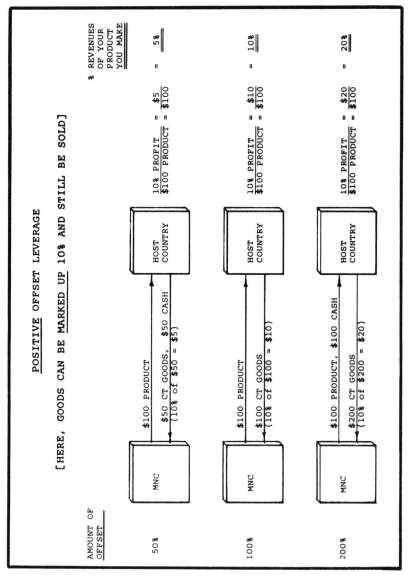

POSITIVE OFFSET LEVERAGE

[HERE, GOODS CAN BE MARKED UP 10% AND STILL BE SOLD]

AMOUNT OF OFFSET

50%

$100 PRODUCT

$50 CT GOODS, $50 CASH
(10% of $50 = $5)

MNC → HOST COUNTRY

$\frac{10\% \text{ PROFIT}}{\$100 \text{ PRODUCT}} = \frac{\$5}{\$100}$

% REVENUES OF YOUR PRODUCT YOU MAKE = 5%

100%

$100 PRODUCT

$100 CT GOODS
(10% of $100 = $10)

MNC → HOST COUNTRY

$\frac{10\% \text{ PROFIT}}{\$100 \text{ PRODUCT}} = \frac{\$10}{\$100}$

= 10%

200%

$100 PRODUCT, $100 CASH

$200 CT GOODS
(10% of $200 = $20)

MNC → HOST COUNTRY

$\frac{10\% \text{ PROFIT}}{\$100 \text{ PRODUCT}} = \frac{\$20}{\$100}$

= 20%

vided the return on investment in the creative countertrade operation is acceptable, larger offsets will produce larger revenues.

The point is that if the MNC can make money on the goods coming back, it can afford to give the host government more than a 100 percent offset. If it allows the host government to recoup its hard currency—and perhaps even allow it some hard currency earnings on the side—two things will happen. First, the host government will be willing to allow the MNC to ship all the products into the country that it can sell there—at least within the constraints of the negotiated countertrade formula. This means the host government will be more willing to make the MNC an exception to those tariff laws that raise the price of products. We see that if the countertrade operation is aggressive and profitable the MNC will get more of its product into the country and sell more once it is there. Hence, creative countertrade gives the MNC commercial leverage with the host government. [Please see Appendix B, which explains the offset formula.]

As an example of what creative countertrade can do, Pepsico reportedly is setting up a fruit processing plant, a seed development facility, and potato and sugar cane processing facilities in India to generate exports with a 300 percent offset ratio. This is in exchange for imports of Pepsi syrup the company wants to sell there.[28] It is unlikely Pepsico would opt for an offset of this size were it taking a loss on the goods coming out of India.

Capital Flow

Creative countertrade increases the flow of capital into the host country for two reasons: (1) by linking imports to exports, it makes investing there more attractive to MNCs and others who might otherwise overlook the opportunities, and (2) by getting the private sector of the Developed World more involved in the investment process, it gives the Third World increased access to international capital markets.

If deals can be established whereby the MNC can make a profit both selling to and exporting from the third world country, MNC interest and investment activity will increase. Once the MNCs realize that creative countertrade can overcome most government restrictions and thus allow them to expand their worldwide sales they will view what was an old problem as a new opportunity and examine their options in earnest.

There is no reason why existing third world enterprises cannot have access to developed world capital markets. Some do. But most do not simply because they lack the required know-how. MNC intervention provides the necessary bridge. Once the MNC provides the seed money and expertise to get a new operation in the host country up and running, it can reduce its risks and expand the operation simultaneously by taking it public on a domestic or a foreign stock exchange. For the host country, the encouragement of this activity will yield a double gain. Increased investment activity in its small business sector is obtained through the provision of increased incentive, and the middle class is strengthened through wider stock ownership.

Creative countertrade can even help ease capital flight, one of the biggest problems third world countries face. The problem is most severe in nations like Argentina, Brazil, Mexico, Nigeria, Peru, Uruguay, and Venezuela. Capital flight in 1984 alone was estimated to be $4 billion from Mexico, $2.2 billion from Brazil, and $2.7 billion from Venezuela.[29] Should creative countertrade take root in these and other countries, the rate of capital flight may well be reduced.

Skill Transfer

Just as creative countertrade will increase capital investment into the Third World, so too will it accelerate the transfer of technology and managerial expertise. Already, production-sharing agreements are being run in many countries. These will continue to expand as firms in developed nations farm out labor-intensive assembly operations to areas where the wage rates are low. In the process, equipment will have to be shipped to the host country, workers have to be trained, and managers have to be educated to run efficient operations. Thus, creative countertrade will accelerate the transfer of skills to the Third World.

Employment and Revenues

In all countries, even the USSR, the small business sector contains the greatest potential for rapid growth in terms of both asset appreciation and employment. Creative countertrade enhances the poten-

Figure 5-12.

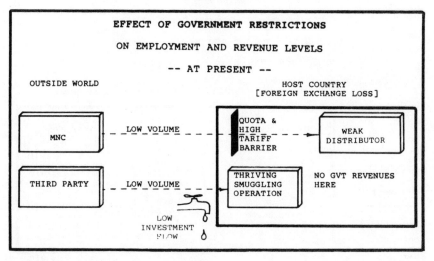

tial of small businesses precisely because that is where the greatest potential return is. Because the growth of small business creates more jobs more quickly than does the expansion of large business, creative countertrade will raise employment levels faster than other programs.

Third world countries became financially ill when they spent excess amounts of their borrowings and foreign exchange earnings on consumption and not enough on capital accumulation. Quotas and high tariffs on consumer products were then instituted to save the third world patient from foreign exchange hemorrhage. Yet while restrictions save the patient, they can be likened to a kind of financial chemotherapy: they poison the nation as well. Figure 5-12 shows the effect quotas and high tariffs have on both the MNC and the host nation.

Restriction of the free flow of products into a country causes market vacuums. It weakens the distributor's position, lowers revenues, and invites smuggling. Most importantly, it does little to increase foreign investment.

By denying its citizens access to desired products at competitive world prices, the host government offers smugglers an irresistibly lucrative market niche, available on the condition that they move their goods without getting caught. Most people suppose that it would make little difference to the MNC how its goods get into the

Figure 5-13.

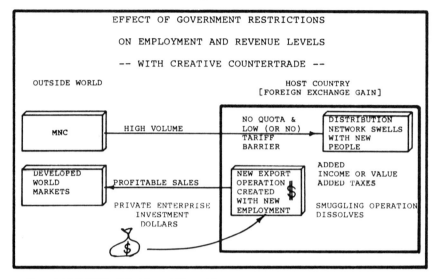

country, legally or otherwise. After all, either way, the MNC gets its money doesn't it? But smuggling is harmful to the MNC because it robs its foreign distributors of the incentive to promote the MNC's products aggressively. Smuggling scoops the cream off the top of the market. Distributors are unwilling to incur the expense and expend the effort required to promote the MNC's product because the customers are buying it for much less in someone else's store. Soon the distributor loses interest, and the product remains on store shelves. Finally, the distributor diversifies and goes after more profitable products.

As Figure 5-13 illustrates, the reduction of product entry restrictions through the use of creative countertrade benefits all involved. Because the legal distribution system swells to accommodate total market demand, the smuggling operation withers, and the black market disappears. Creative countertrade means higher volumes for the MNC, more jobs for the local population, and added revenues for the host government. Creative countertrade is supply-side economics at its best, effected without draining hard cash reserves of the third world country.

Let's view the situation from a different perspective for a moment. In a way, quotas and tariffs are like a government-built dam that pro-

Figure 5-14.

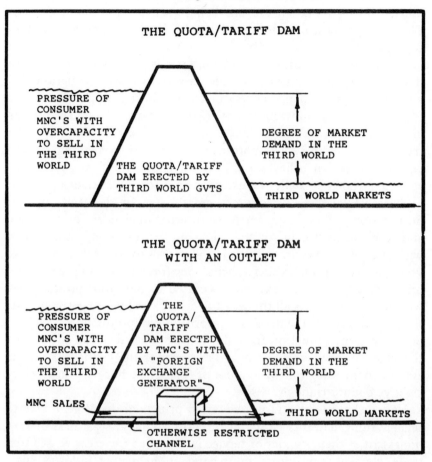

hibits excluded products from entering the host country (top of Figure 5-14). But the best way to prevent foreign exchange hemorrhage is simply to let the local currency float freely in the world market. Equilibrium will quickly be reached and the outflow will be stopped. Free trade—by far the easiest and most efficient kind— would flourish and prosperity would soon follow.

However, many third world governments do not allow their currencies to float freely because of the political cost of attendant inflation. Rather, they keep them high while restricting the inflow of "nonessential" items. The effect is to reduce the comparative cost of essential items by increasing the street cost of consumer items.

According to this philosophy the dam had to be built in order to prevent foreign exchange from being used for nonessential items. The dam, meanwhile, does nothing. It simply perpetuates a static situation.

On the other hand, creative countertrade in exchange for the reduction of quotas and tariffs, called a selective tariff reduction, provides a foreign exchange generator for the host country (bottom of Figure 5-14). By allowing the MNC to earmark some of the net foreign exchange to sell its products more easily within the host country, the host country gets unrestricted use of the remaining net foreign exchange. In other words, the MNC and the host government agree in advance to *share* the use of the net foreign exchange.

Selective tariff reductions can greatly benefit the MNC and the host country alike. They increase international sales for the MNC and foreign investment for the host country. Essentially, the nation with the selective tariff reduction policy says to the MNC, "Provided you can expand our exports—hence our foreign exchange earnings—more than the foreign exchange we used to buy your products, we will drop your tariffs all the way to zero, if need be, to get you to do this regardless of the level of priority your products now have." Selective tariff reduction formulas can be worked out in advance by the host country whereby it agrees to lower the tariff by a certain amount depending on the amount of foreign exchange it earns in the creative countertrade process.

Under the selective tariff reduction principle, the MNC is free to sell anything it wants to sell in the host country, regardless of how nonessential that product or service is, provided the creative countertrade element can create or expand an exporting industry by a greater foreign exchange amount. By removing stiff tariffs from those specific consumer products tied to creative countertrade, the host country expands investment incentive to include a large developed world economic engine heretofore stymied: the consumer product industry.

By offering MNCs increased import rights and selective tariff reductions, third world governments use the sales pressure from MNCs to market products within their borders and thereby expand their export sectors. The benefits are open to MNCs willing to help the third world country solve its particular problems.

The Tariff Problem

Of the two problems—generating foreign exchange and reducing tariffs—the tariff problem is the more difficult to solve. Tariff adjustments in any country have always been highly charged, political issues. For this reason, people at all levels treat the subject gingerly.

Often, when MNCs petition for lower tariffs, government officials treat the request with a considerable degree of skepticism, if not suspicion. "What's the catch?" they ask. They scrutinize the proposal to see if the petitioner is gaining any unfair or hidden advantage, or if the government's policies might in any way be compromised. A second impediment is that tariffs are usually written into law and thus cannot be changed at the ministerial or bureaucratic level. In many instances, tariff changes require a policy decision at the highest level and legislative action. In the meantime, government functionaries simply shrug even if they are in perfect agreement with the idea. Therefore, it is unlikely an MNC salesman clad in a woolen suit and wing tips is going to waltz into a government office and tell the agent there to make it snappy lowering the tariff because he doesn't have all day. Things just are not done like that. Nor will the level of the office he visits, nor the amount of hat-in-hand do him much good either.

At the same time, tariffs are not written in stone. They *can* be and *are* being changed. For example, in December 1984, Alcoa Aluminum signed a long-term commitment with Brazil's Commission for the Concession of Fiscal Benefits to Special Export Programs (BEFIEX), through which Alcoa's Brazilian subsidiary will enjoy as much as 90 percent duty reductions on imported equipment and raw material. In return, Brazil will gain a sizeable increase in its net exports through creative countertrade. Alcoa and a consortium of nine other companies were able to get the Brazilian government to agree to this proposal due to its sheer size: $2.7 billion worth of exports over the next 15 years from which Brazil will receive a $500 million trade surplus.[30]

On a smaller transaction scale the same principle works, and selective tariff reduction provides the host government with, relatively speaking, equivalent benefits. Provided governmental machinery is able to handle a large number of selective tariff reduction transactions, the sum total of those transactions could net the host country exports equal or exceeding the Alcoa deal. If government administrators ensure that each transaction earns the country more exports than it costs it in imports, the rest should take care of itself.

Selective tariff reduction should not be viewed as a form of special treatment for a particular MNC, but rather a matter of public policy beneficial to the host government. Under such public policy, across-the-board selective tariff reduction could be open to any MNC facing high tariffs and willing to engage in creative countertrade.

Tariff Revenues

Just because a government decides to lower tariffs does not necessarily mean that it will lose tariff revenues in the process. Figure 5-15 illustrates how an increase in volume will allow a third world government to earn equivalent revenues at a reduced tariff level.

Many people criticize supply-side economics in the United States because the positive effects of reduced taxes on the economy are unpredictable. But with creative countertrade the offset ratio can be worked out precisely in advance. The government is in almost a risk-

Figure 5-15.

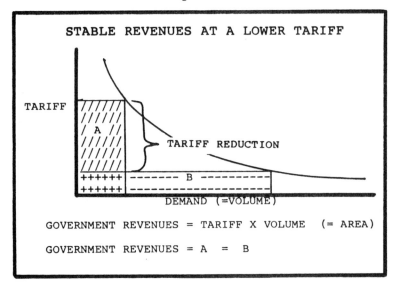

free posture, because tariff reduction hinges on the success of the countertrade operation.

Under the selective tariff reduction formula, the tariff could be reduced to zero as the domestic value added of the countertraded goods exported from the country approached a predetermined or negotiated percent of the value of the MNC's products imported. An important factor to consider in these negotiations is what percent of the total cost of the *countertraded goods* is domestic value added content. The MNC must have good accounting figures here, as the host country may try to low-ball it. Also important is what percent of the value of the *MNC's product* is the domestic value added content of the countertraded goods.

Although it may look as though the host government holds all the cards, actually, it does not. The outcome depends on the relative desire of each side to complete a deal. However, governments may be more inclined to deadlock, as government officials are more often judged not on their successes but on their mistakes.

Foreign Control

Of all the forms of investment, creative countertrade allows for the highest levels of local ownership and control as these issues are not essential ingredients of a successful creative countertrade equation.

Infant industries are not only protected, they are expanded by people who know how to run business the best. Although MNCs may initially play a dominant role, third world governments can protect themselves from long-term domination by outside interests simply by specifying at the outset the number of years (10 to 20 in most cases) after which control is to revert completely to the domestic owners. The MNC requires neither ownership nor control in order to assure that the terms of the creative countertrade contract are met. Thus, foreign control of industry will be kept to a minimum.

CONSTRAINTS OF CREATIVE COUNTERTRADE

As is the case with traditional countertrade, so too are there constraints to creative countertrade. Some of them have to do with the business philosophy of the MNC itself. Creative countertrade usually requires the MNC to become more involved with the Third World; therefore, the constraints of doing business in the Third World necessarily become the constraints of conducting creative countertrade.

MNC and Third World Reservations

Some executives may not wish to make the commitment of two to three years needed to develop an export industry in a third world country. Although rarely profitable, they may prefer ad-hoc countertrade because it requires a much lower level of involvement. Those companies, however, doing ad-hoc countertrade every year, may well be inclined to consider a more permanent investment.

Managers may resist creative countertrade because they claim it falls outside their area of expertise. "We're in the left-handed screwdriver business," they declare. "What do we know about starting strange businesses in far-off countries?" MNC managers may be justified in their concerns, but less justified than they think. If the MNC wants to sell its left-handed screw drivers into a particular country and cannot do so without countertrade, it is going to have to think of something or else give up the market.

The corporation does not necessarily have to leave its line of business in order to do creative countertrade. In fact, the closer it stays to some aspect of it, the more successful it may be. The MNC should only consider unrelated lines of business when it spots a lucrative opportunity or when it has no related alternatives. However, more entrepreneurial MNCs who refuse to wrap themselves in preconceived self-images of who they are and what they do, may be more successful setting up operations geared toward moving their traditional products abroad.

Many large MNCs have proven track records of diversifying into new areas. Moreover, if the MNC choses a line of creative countertrade that lends itself to trade with a wide number of third world countries, it can afford to develop the needed businesses expertise and thus compete successfully. When the MNC is interested but has little expertise in certain lines of business, joint ventures can be established with experienced businesses.

Third world countries may object to creative countertrade on the basis that it is unfair to companies already established there. "It will open a Pandora's box of problems," they might assert. "It would greatly complicate our lives." "Every Tom, Dick and MNC in our country will be down on us to get countertrade credits," they could complain. "It will eat up all our cash sales. Besides," they may say, "we will lose valuable revenues from tariffs." But third world countries do not have to permit creative countertrade. There is nothing that says they have to have a selective reduction of their tariffs or that they have to do anything. But if they do not, they may wind up losing business to those of their neighbors who do. Pandora's box may already be open wider than they think. Increasingly MNCs are demanding from third world nations countertrade credits for what used to be cash purchases.

Ironically some third world countries already engaged in countertrade resist creative countertrade because of potential administrative problems. In the long run, the ongoing nature of creative countertrade poses *less* of an administrative burden to the host government, than do traditional countertrade arrangements.

The argument about the loss of tariff revenues makes no sense when the low volume of imports renders tariff revenue negligible. Similarly, no value-added tax revenue is generated on the transaction because there is no counterbusiness.

All of this is not to say that third world governments should not carefully examine creative countertrade and selective tariff reduction. But to reject the concept out of hand because it does not have a seat on the national political bandwagon would be short-sighted.

Difficulties of Doing Business in the Third World

Even if the host government is totally cooperative, setting up a productive operation in another country is never easy. Some of the problems include:

1. Low managerial skills among some of the workforce, specifically, poor organization, risk of production schedules not being met, low technical expertise, illiteracy, slower life-style, and incompatible work ethic
2. Lack of sound physical facilities, including dilapidated buildings, no air conditioning, run down or no machines, and not enough trucks; and a fledgling infrastructure, including few surfaced

roads, unreliable electric power, lack of potable water, and few good sewage treatment plants

3. Long distances between the MNC and the host country, presenting the following problems: heightened transportation and freight costs, travel and per diem expenses going both ways, and the impediments of psychological distance

4. Cultural and linguistic barriers on both sides to be overcome

5. Governmental problems, including political instability; suspicious, overly intrusive, bureaucratic and uncooperative officials; inability to obtain sufficient foreign exchange to pay for imported parts, etc.; and lack of knowledge of business fundamentals which inhibit commercial activity

6. Marketing problems, specifically an ignorance of distant markets, highly skilled competition in the developed world, and competition familiar with the foreign marketplace

On the other hand, the Third World offers these advantages:

1. Low labor wage rates
2. Rapidly increasing labor skill levels
3. Proximity to third world markets
4. Closeness to sources of raw materials and cheaper energy
5. Rapidly expanding industrial bases—especially in newly industrialized countries
6. Rapid increase in technical skills and organizational ability
7. Economic growth rates with a potential for much greater growth than that in developed world economies
8. Countertrade credits that could be offered to MNCs making luxury, or "nonessential," products and to consumer product MNCs.

NOTES

1. Some observers may object that the term *creative countertrade* is a bit of a misnomer, in that countertrade is creative to begin with. As with anything, the creativity involved is relative. Countertrade has been around for a while, and the term *creative countertrade* aptly describes new types of countertrade transactions.

2. The North can be roughly defined as the First World (consisting of the rich nations of Japan, the United States, Canada, and the nations of Western

Europe) and the Second World (consisting of the Soviet Union and the socialist countries of Eastern Europe), both of which are situated for the most part above the equator. The South can be defined as the poorer countries near or below the equator. Although the Middle East has a history of interaction with Europe, many parts of it have social and economic problems that are similar to other poorer countries of the South. For a superb description of the similarities and differences among the world countries, see Pluto Press, *The New State of the World Atlas*, (New York, Simon & Schuster, 1984). One hour with this book will give the reader more insight into the state of the world than reading a week's worth of articles.

3.   Peter F. Drucker, "The Changed World Economy," *Foreign Affairs Quarterly* 64, no. 4 (Spring 1986): 768.

4.   James R. Norman, Todd Mason, Sandra D. Atchison, John N. Frank, and Patrick Houston, "America's Deflation Belt," *Business Week*, June 9, 1986, p. 54.

5.   Drucker, "The Changed World Economy," p. 768.

6.   Ibid.

7.   Despite the fact that Japan is the most heavily automated nation in the world, over a half million jobs are expected to be lost to overseas investment by the year 2000. Leslie Helm, "Japan Is Paying for Its Strong Yen—In Jobs," *Business Week*, June 9, 1986, p. 47.

8.   Drucker, "The Changed World Economy," p. 769.

9.   Julian Weiss, "High-Tech Lets Third World Outdo West in Key Skills," *Christian Science Monitor*, May 20, 1986, p. 24.

10. Weiss, "High-Tech Lets Third World Outdo West."

11. John C. Griffin, Jr., and William Rouse, "Countertrade as a Third World Strategy of Development," *Third World Quarterly* (January 1986): 177–204.

12. *Countertrade Outlook*, July 15, 1985, p. 2; Griffin and Rousse, "Countertrade as a Third World Strategy."

13. *Countertrade Outlook*, April 29, 1985, p. 2.

14. Fred Tarter, "Countertrade—the Corporate Experience," Countertrade Seminar, World Trade Center, New York, N.Y., December 16–17, 1985.

15. *Countertrade Outlook*, December 9, 1985, p. 1.

16. This chapter, however, examines the restraints from the point of view of MNCs engaged in smaller sales, in which case the primary restraints are quotas and tariffs.

17. Everett G. Martin and Thomas E. Ricks, "Countertrading Grows and Cash Short Nations Seek Marketing Help," *Wall Street Journal*, March 13, 1985, p. 1.

18. *Countertrade Outlook*, August 18, 1983, p. 2.

19. Dave Griffiths, "A 'Shield' the Saudis Will Use to Police the Gulf," *Business Week*, February 18, 1985, pp. 138E–F; "Boeing Aerospace Wins Bid

for Saudi Air Defense," *Aviation Week*, March 4, 1985, p. 23; Richard G. O'Lone, "Boeing, Saudi Arabia Tie Defense System to Economic Package," *Aviation Week*, January 3, 1985, p. 155; *Countertrade Outlook*, March 18, 1985, p. 1.

20. O'Lone, "Boeing, Saudi Arabia Tie."

21. *Countertrade Outlook*, September 26, 1983, p. 2.

22. *Countertrade Outlook*, April 29, 1985, p. 2.

23. *Countertrade Outlook*, August 20, 1984, p. 2.

24. Robert D. Schmidt, "On High Technology Trade," *Government Executive*, April 1981, pp. 20, 22.

25. Willis Bussard, "A View of Countertrade" (Princeton, N.J., 1983, unpublished study).

26. Raveed and Renforth, "State Enterprise–MNC Joint Ventures: How Well Do They Meet Both Partners' Needs?" *Management International Review* 23, no. 1 (1983): 47.

27. Audley Shaw (Director, North America, Jamaica National Investment Promotion Limited), interview with author, December 1984.

28. *Countertrade Outlook*, December 23, 1985, p. 6.

29. Gary Hector, "Nervous Money Keeps on Fleeing," *Fortune*, December 23, 1983, pp. 103–104.

30. James Bruce, "Brazil's Export Commitments Top $85 Billion," *Journal of Commerce* (December 12, 1984): 5A.

6 CREATIVE COUNTERTRADE STRATEGY

To establish a creative countertrade operation companies must first persuade the host government to agree to the plan. Many companies regard the host government as their adversary. When they approach the proposed arrangement strictly with a "What's in it for me?" mentality, the host government tends to respond similarly, often refusing to cooperate and smothering the MNC in red tape. If, on the other hand, the MNC convinces the government it is sensitive to its interests and willing to listen, the MNC has a much better chance of getting government cooperation. MNCs must offer the host government economic and political incentives if the proposed venture is to succeed.

THE GAME PLAN

The MNC should first determine which countries are blocking the importation of its products,[1] and second, examine the possible effect of lower tariffs on the company's import volume.

Price/Volume Relationship

In a country with a long history of established tariffs, it is impossible to ascertain what effect a reduction in tariffs and the consequent reduction of the street price of products will have on the MNC's sales. As tariffs on many products hover close to 100 percent of their F.O.B. value, a tariff elimination might mean a 50 percent reduction in the street price. Although it is difficult to tell how much volume would expand under these circumstances, it is possible that the incremental increase could be significant. While it is important to know the size of the existing market and tariff rates for each country, it is equally important to estimate how these markets will change as tariff rates drop. It is conceivable that a large market in one country would change less than a smaller one in another country. Considerations such as these will, therefore, influence location decisions.

Once a selection of a handful of countries has been made, the next task is to determine the countries where the most successful creative countertrade operations might be launched while considering potential countries, MNCs should also scan markets in the developed world for niches and opportunities.

For proposed Caribbean business ventures, Production Sharing International, Ltd., a consulting firm based in Southport, Connecticut, has developed a computerized Investment Decision Grid™ to help client investors. The grid weights by country such factors as economic, social and political stability, labor characteristics, transportation issues, extent of the service infrastructure, degree of government cooperation, amount of favorable treatment by developed world markets, and quality of life.[2] Other consulting firms do the same thing, although much of this information is available either free or at low cost from the U.S. government, public institutions, and consulates of the countries themselves.

Fortunately, those countries with the greatest opportunities for creative countertrade deals are usually those with the largest markets. All the newly industrialized countries (NICs) are candidates. Some specific countries are:

1. Argentina
2. Brazil
3. China
4. Colombia
5. India
6. Israel
7. Jamaica
8. Mexico
9. South Africa

Low-Tech/Services

Although it is often advised that a company stick to its product area of expertise, this does not mean that companies have to automatically rule out consideration of other types of business. For high-tech MNCs, high-tech projects are a natural route, and certainly markets exist for their projects. But there are a number of reasons why both the MNC and the host country might want to consider as projects low-tech and the service industries.[3] As profitable diversification can run in a surprising number of directions, the presence or absence of high technology need not be the over-riding criterion in the decisionmaking process.

Opportunities for the transfer of an MNC's own technology to a third world country are often limited. The MNC may be unwilling to transfer a closely-held technology. The technology may still be in the R&D phase and thus require too much at-home support to get it working. Or the technology may require so much production machinery that it cannot be economically transferred to the Third World. Sometimes high success rates and dollar volumes are generated more quickly when high technology is bypassed. The MNC risk is lower, the lead times to market are shorter, and flexibility is maximized.

Low tech and service businesses make the best use of available resources. They tend to be labor-intensive; most of them use cheap or few materials; and strong market niches can be created for them in the developed world. Without big plants with lots of equipment to worry about, warehouses of inventory to sell, or huge costs to write off, these businesses can be easily closed if they do not work. Moreover, others can be brought in to share the risk.[4] Once a business team becomes skilled at starting up a service or low-tech business in one foreign country, it can expand its operations to nearby countries. Since, in many cases, working and living conditions are similar throughout geographical regions, the business expertise gained in one area can easily be transferred and converted to a neighboring country's needs.[5]

In fact, many of mainland China's projects are directly applicable to other parts of the Third World. The Chinese are becoming so adept at maximizing private foreign investment that both MNCs and other third world nations would do well to watch them carefully.[6]

In addition, low tech and service-oriented creative countertrade may be more lucrative than traditional high-tech plant transfer because of lower costs, lower risk, speed of market entry, and fewer patent problems.

There are fewer R&D expenditures, either technical or business, in low tech and service ventures. Either the products already exist in sample form or they will be modifications of existing products. Capital expenditures are lower. The equipment either already exists or is cheap to procure. Less training is required than would be for a high-tech venture. Most of the needed expertise is either available or easily taught. Administrative expense can be reduced because the ventures do not require extensive engineering support. Moreover, no highly skilled scientists or engineers will have to be pulled off existing projects to work on this new one. The risk is lower. The MNC does not necessarily have to run the business itself. Instead, it can let others do it as in a joint venture, licensing, or other contractual arrangement. Its partner can be either a national from the host country or someone from the outside. Market entry tends to be faster, thus promising a more speedy potential payoff. Low tech/service allows the MNC to generate revenues and get the countertrade process started more quickly, which benefits all concerned. Finally, there are no esoteric patents to fight over. The products will either no longer be under patent protection or else be simply unpatentable, thus lessening the risk of protracted court battles.

JOINT VENTURES

Joint venture partners are worthwhile because they can usually tell at the outset whether an idea is worthwhile, they can defray the investment expense and the risk, they know the market, and can help with production setup and training. For an American MNC, an American partner has an added advantage of being contracted with under U.S. law. Other firms, either in the developed or the Third World, might be willing to enter joint ventures especially if they are too small to set up a profitable venture alone.

If the potential partner believes it could increase its own revenues/profits (perhaps substantially) or reduce production costs, it certainly will be interested. The MNC could provide free help enabling the partner to gain international exposure. Provided the MNC gets the countertrade credits and recovers some of its expenses, it may even be willing to let the joint venture partner have a greater share of the profits than would otherwise be the case.

Who Uses Joint Ventures?

According to a survey of executives of over 150 MNCs, most of the Fortune 500 companies and about 40 percent of industrial firms with sales exceeding $100 million are involved in at least one international joint venture.[7] Half of the new international joint ventures begun since 1980 were motivated, at least in part, by the desire of MNCs in mature markets to enter "attractive new markets." Over a third were motivated by a desire to deal with awakening economic nationalism, which restricts foreign ownership of assets.[8]

Luis Monge, past president of Costa Rica, has declared that over a dozen Minnesota-based companies alone have established joint ventures in his country.[9] The Spire Corporation of Bedford, MA, makes turnkey solar cell manufacturing plants for third world countries. As of late 1983, Spire had franchises in Brazil, Tunisia, and India and joint ventures in Saudi Arabia and Egypt, thus assuring that photovoltaics will be a growth industry for years to come.[10]

Caterpillar Tractor Company is considering both countertrade and joint ventures overseas due to a strong dollar, tough international competition, and the inability of third world countries to pay for earth moving machinery.[11] The U.S. chemical industry is examining increased use of international joint ventures in an effort to remain financially viable.[12]

A growing number of MNCs are setting up third world joint ventures in much the same way they began joint ventures in the Low Countries after the start of the Common Market. They intend to establish bases of operations in Central and South America and in South East Asia in order to develop new markets, keep up with the competition, and increase export opportunities.[13]

Types of Joint Ventures

The term, joint venture, implies shared equity and management between legal business entities (i.e., not persons). Parties enter joint ventures to obtain such things as lower risk, finance, managerial expertise, technical skills, marketing connections, and trade barriers. The MNC can establish joint ventures with a number of other entities in six basic types of agreements:[14] (1) marketing and distribution, (2) patent and trademark, (3) licensing, (4) management contract, (5) overseas division or subsidiary, and (6) creation of a separate joint venture entity.

In general, the greater the motivation and opportunity for contact between parties, the greater the likelihood of a joint venture.[15] Joint ventures normally work best when one member is clearly in control; shared control works best when both sides share managerial input. Early success will keep a joint venture alive;[16] Planning and mutual trust will keep start-up problems at a minimum. The advice of tax counsel is essential.[17]

According to Barbara Cannon, president of Cannon Consulting, a California-based international marketing consulting firm, joint ventures have the following advantages and disadvantages:

Advantages	Disadvantages
Preferential treatment by host government	Reduced overall profit
Reduced capital investment	Reduced managerial control over operations
Lower political and economic risk	Unequal investment of resources by partners
Immediate market access	Creation of possible future competitor
Second sourcing for products	Risk of nationalization
Increased international exposure	Problems working with foreign partner.[18]

Most businesses regard joint ventures as long-term commitments because they require so much effort. However, many governments— especially socialist ones—see joint ventures as temporary stepping stones for getting enterprises built and working. Accommodation between businesses and the host government, however, may not be difficult because a relatively long time-span for a business (15 to 20 years) may be regarded by certain governments as a relatively short one.

Setting Up a Joint Venture

There are many ways to set up international joint ventures and a wealth of literature explains them. What follows is an explanation of how international joint venturing and creative countertrade can be combined.

Figure 6–1 depicts how creative countertrade can be done with a joint venture partner. In the lower part of the diagram, the MNC

Figure 6–1.

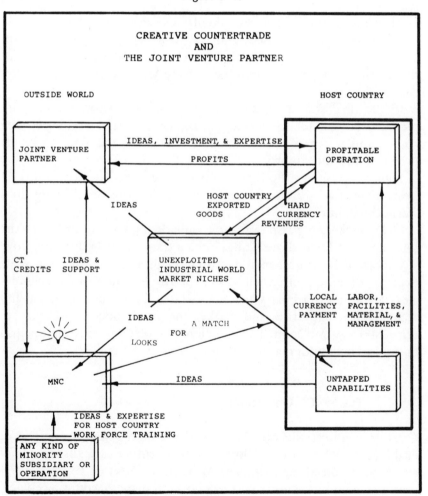

searches for ideas in the same manner it did in the feasibility study. Using its expertise, it tries to spot market niches that can be filled from host country sources.

The MNC tries its ideas out on potential joint venture partners— either outside or inside the host country—to see if there is interest. An alternative approach would be to ask if potential partners have ideas of their own they would like help developing.

Well in advance of setting up the operation, the MNC must succeed in getting the host government to grant it countertrade credits for import licenses and selective tariff reductions to sell its products in the country.

The fourth stage includes takeoff and revenue building. Break-even volumes are surpassed, and the firm begins to make a profit. The joint venture partner, of course, enjoys repatriation of some of the profits after partially reimbursing the MNC for its out-of-pocket costs.

In the final step a certain percentage of the export revenues are recorded in an evidence account in the central bank as countertrade credits and selective tariff reductions that allow the MNC to get its products into the country.

Figure 6–1 shows the first four steps together. The key to success is an innovative search for market needs that can be filled by third world capabilities.

McDonnell–Douglas has already embarked on a plan similar to the four steps outlined above. It has hired a trader to help Spain improve a number of its export manufacturing facilities and thus increase its exports. Because McDonnell lacks expertise in a number of technologies, it is using third party investors who will transfer managerial and technological expertise, and market the goods once exported. Another strategy McDonnell has explored is offering existing Spanish businesses help with marketing their wares overseas.[19]

The MNC's Operations

Creative countertrade can make good use of the MNC's operations, enabling the MNC to act as both a limited venture capitalist company and a giant consulting firm. The MNC is in a position to offer entrepreneurs and joint venture partners business plans, accounting advice, and credit checks from its finance department; research, forecasting, and advertising advice from marketing; sales channel information and hands-on advice about American and international retailers from sales; warehousing, shipping, and order entry help from distribution; and manufacturing guidance from engineering and production.

Experience in plants located in depressed U.S. urban areas may transfer superbly to foreign countries. The objective is to use existing personnel and facilities in ways that do not hinder their current work. Setting up a consultancy situation in which MNC management helps others may actually give managers new perspectives and improve their management skills.

USING OUTSIDE HELP

Ex-Peace Corps Volunteers

A high percentage of Peace Corps volunteers have liberal arts degrees. Often, in spite of their talent and a wealth of knowledge gained overseas, they have difficulty finding good paying and satisfying employment when they re-enter the workplace in the United States. Perhaps MNCs and ex-Peace Corps volunteers can join forces. Often MNCs are hard put to find managers willing to live in third world countries for the extended periods necessary to oversee new operations. Often there are adjustment problems and disappointments on all sides. Sometimes their people return after discovering they could not bridge the cultural barriers. Ex-Peace Corps volunteers willing to remain in a culture to which they have already become acculturated may be available in exchange for higher pay, business training, and a brighter career prospects.[20]

Outside Financial Sources

Money is available for third world business from:

1. U.S. AID
2. EXIM Bank
3. Individuals inside the host country
4. Local entrepreneurs
5. International banks

6. International venture capital firms
7. Other companies in the developed world
8. Individuals in the developed world
9. Stock exchanges

Sometimes, the MNC would act as an investor, sometimes in the capacity of a broker/facilitator. For instance, an MNC-sponsored small business in a third world country may use the MNC's staff expertise and contacts to raise capital through stock or bond offerings in the Developed World. For most small businesses in the Third World such a course of action would be next to impossible without assistance.

U.S. AID.   The U.S. AID (Agency for International Development) Office has helped a number of small businesses in the Third World get financing. U.S. AID normally awards grants on a government-to-government basis. In other words, the host government sponsors particular projects; the U.S. AID office gives the money to the host government; and the host government then transfers the money to the projects. American MNCs that undertake joint ventures with local firms may be eligible for this financing.[21]

OPIC.   OPIC (Overseas Private Investment Corporation) in Washington D.C. provides financing for American business in 100 third world countries. Direct loans of $100,000 to $4,000,000 are available to small businesses (not on the Fortune 1000) at 1.5 percent to 3.0 percent interest for up to 50 percent of the project.

In 1981, OPIC lent Jamaica Broilers $1 million to expand its poultry farm at White Marl, Jamaica. Now, the company processes about 60 percent of the chicken consumed by the country. Although a Jamaican company, Jamaica Broilers qualified for the OPIC financing because it purchases its equipment, breeder eggs, and feed grain from small businesses in the United States.[22]

Caribbean Basin Initiative (CBI).   The CBI makes imports into the United States from Caribbean nations duty free if the manufacturer in the Caribbean country has added at least 35 percent local value-added to the product. This lowers to 20 percent if 15 percent of the product has been produced inside the United States or its territories.

The goods are shipped directly from the host country to a U.S. city. Over 2,800 items enter the United States duty free under this program.

Recent news articles indicate the CBI has run aground in Congress. However, Congress only reneged in the textile area. There are four major exclusions from CBI:

- Textiles
- Tuna fish
- Footwear, especially safety shoes
- Oil

For the most part other goods come into the United States duty free.

STRATEGIC ALTERNATIVES

Production sharing: part of a product is made in one country and part of it is made or assembled in another country. Parts have been assembled for years in Asia, where labor has been cheap. But now, production sharing is moving to the Caribbean where countries like Haiti, the Dominican Republic, and El Salvador can provide hard working, low-cost labor.

Under the GSP (Generalized System of Preferences) components for the MNC's products may enter many countries of the developed world with reduced tariffs as long as 35 percent of their value has been added in most of the Third World. For American companies, the CBI (Caribbean Basin Initiative) offers even greater tariff advantages as only 20 percent of the value has to be added in the Caribbean as long as at least 15 percent is added in the United States.

Many MNCs already have their own production and production-sharing facilities running in third world countries. In all probability it would be difficult for them to get countertrade credits for these installations. However, if they were to expand their operations and allow a number of smaller companies with production sharing of their own to piggyback onto them, the expense to the MNCs would be minimal, but the countertrade credits derived could well be substantial.

According to articles in *Countertrade Outlook*, Xerox, using Brazil as a springboard, has become a major contender in creative countertrade around the world. When Xerox incurred a 10 percent discount on a $2 million soybeans-to-India deal with Brazil in 1981, management decided that traditional countertrade was not viable in the long run. The first thing Xerox did was to open a local trading company called EXPRO in order to get government discounts and other forms of favorable treatment given to local business. EXPRO's primary purpose is to act as a liaison between the worldwide distribution and marketing network and those able to source goods and materials from Brazilian manufacturers. Additionally, EXPRO searches out and helps Brazilian manufacturers upgrade their products to meet export standards.

But Xerox did not stop there. The next thing it did was to look for small importers and companies in other parts of the world that would in the normal course of their business purchase Brazilian products, thus expediting the movement of goods from Brazilian sources.

EXPRO exported over $10 million worth of Brazilian goods within the first year of its operation. In 1984, it exported almost $75 million worth of Brazilian goods in contrast to Xerox Brazil, which only imported $40 million worth of goods the prior year. Today, almost two-thirds of the goods EXPRO ships from Brazil are related to Xerox products and can be used either in-house or sold through the company's worldwide marketing and distribution system. They include such things as paper, pulp, parts, machines, toner, and developer; the remaining exports consist of steel, processed food, tin, and manufactured products.[23]

The MNC, acting as a catalyst as in the case of Xerox with EXPRO, can forge a direct link between the Third World and the small non-international businesses in other parts of the world, which are the Third World's fastest growth sector. MNCs can give hands-on industrial manufacturing help to small companies, and this with a minimum of expense and delay, while providing host countries a bonanza of increased business.

The result is an upward business spiral. In part, through the help of EXPRO, Brazil has become the world's fourth largest exporter of pulp. The more small businesses assemble products in the Third World, the lower their costs and the better their ability to compete. Assembly work done in the Third World allows for increased foreign exchange, and thus increased buying power. When the Third World buys more, MNCs can sell more. Everybody benefits.

The methodology is not difficult. If plastic molding and metal fabricating facilities were set up in a third world country along with a good hand assembly operation, the MNC managing these facilities would be well positioned. The value added from the fabrication could be added to the value added from the assembly, thus helping the product to qualify for tariff-free treatment under the GSP or CBI. Once the MNC had attended to its own production needs, it could package its idle capacity for use by small businesses in the developed world, giving them international exposure and economies of scale equivalent to that of large corporations.

Other creative countertrade alternatives follow:

Vacation Real Estate

The MNC could arrange for a third party to invest in a hotel in the host country. The third party would receive the profits, after the MNC's expenses are paid, and the MNC gets the countertrade credits. For example, a plush downhill ski resort in the Chinese Himalayas could target as their market the jetset rich, for high prices and high margins. Downhill skiing in China would appeal to the large number of high-level executives and government officials from developed world countries who travel to China for business, thus making China a superb getaway place for both business and relaxation purposes. The resort could in turn be used by Chinese marketers as a showcase demonstrating an imaginative plan on the part of a foreign company to generate foreign exchange and penetrate the Chinese market.

A joint venture between a large U.S. manufacturer and a company such as Hilton, Hyatt, or Marriott might prove to be a workable combination. Perhaps even a consortium of manufacturers and hotel chains would do, with the manufacturers and hotel companies sharing investment costs, risk, and negotiating responsibilities. The hotel companies would additionally provide the necessary design, real estate, and managerial input needed to make the venture work.

As many building materials and most labor would be Chinese, construction costs would be lower than in the West, but hotel bills and meals would not. All parties would share in the hard-currency proceeds until at some later date (perhaps fifteen to twenty years) the resort would be fully owned by the Chinese.

Data Entry Services

Using its entrepreneurial resources, the MNC could establish a U.S. company providing fast, low-cost key punching and typing services to be done in the host country. Like the Deerfield Communications keypunching firm, Control Data has set up a joint venture key punch firm in Jamaica. Not only does the firm handle Control Data's needs, it does keypunching for a number of other firms as well, and for less than it would cost in the United States. American Airlines also has an operation in the Caribbean for its own use. There are a number of possibilities in this regard.

Database Services

In a related area, there is a growing need for specific bibliographic data base information about foreign countries. It is not available, primarily because most of the publications are written in foreign languages. A clipping, abstracting, and translating house in Brazil and Mexico that sold computer tapes to such companies as DIALOG, Dow Jones, or the SOURCE, could be set up quickly and inexpensively, and generate substantial funds.

Increasing Agricultural Output

The MNC does not necessarily need to increase net exports for creative countertrade to work. It can also reduce net imports. Because of its vast growth potential, agriculture offers many possibilities. Many third world countries possess rich agricultural resources, but are not utilizing them efficiently because of lack of organization and know-how.

Even a non-agricultural MNC could do something in this area. By paying an agricultural team of experts to organize and train local farmers, the MNC could negotiate with the host government to be given credits on a contingent basis depending on the degree of increase in the farmers' yields. As some of its expenses may qualify the MNC for aid from the U.S. and other governments, and as the percentage increase in crop yields can run as high as several hundred percent, within in very short period agricultural creative countertrade could prove highly profitable. In effect, the MNC would create a kind of private enterprise similar to the Peace Corps operation. As agricultural output by small farmers is a high priority item in most third world countries, any kind of proposition along these lines should generate considerable interest. Moreover, agribusiness techniques learned in one country are highly transferable to others.

Turnkey Plants

Turnkey plants are an excellent way for the MNC to both recoup its investment and get countertrade credits. China, especially, has become a world leader in facilitating turnkey facilities within its borders. A careful study of the way the Chinese are handling turnkey operations may facilitate the installation of similar operations in other third world countries. Hong Kong has handled over 5,000 countertrade deals with China, many of which have been small buy-back deals. Yet to date, no study has been made as to specifically what these deals are and how they have been carried out.

Limestone Carvings

Ornate facades carved in limestone on old buildings have disappeared from modern architecture largely because craftsmen's wages made this work too expensive. Most third world countries have carving expertise, but in wood rather than stone. The Filipinos, for example, are very good with wooden carvings.

Why couldn't an MNC help a third world country convert its wood-carving talents to limestone facades to be sold to contractors and architects in the developed world? Architects in the developed world could be notified of the possibilities and costs of such a venture. After designing the patterns they wished to appear on the walls, the architects could confer with a representative of the limestone carving company, submit their plans, and have them replicated in stone slabs that would then be crated and shipped to the construction site at the prescribed time.[24]

Educational Television

The geosynchronous satellite; photovoltaics; and the low cost, low-power color television will greatly accelerate the sale and use of television in third world countries within the next fifteen years. The market for locally produced self-help educational television programs will grow exponentially. Conversely, demand for film footage of third world countries in the developed world will increase in future years as the realization spreads that the future of the both worlds are inseparably linked.

One potential market includes joint ventures between public television stations in the developed world and third world universities and communications people for the purpose of creating such programs. With funds from U.S. AID, the World Bank, and other agencies, the MNC could use blocked funds and be reimbursed in hard currency.

Reconditioning of Old Cars and Appliances

Two other ideas that could be used to create foreign exchange in third world countries are the repair and refurbishment of old automobiles and of small appliances. Why should any third world nation pay retail for its cars and appliances, when it could get just as good ones for a fraction of the price? Americans throw away everything from the toaster to the television. Many times these items are in fairly good condition. The United States has no business establishment that refurbishes cars and appliances on a large scale.

A country wishing to set up purchasing centers in major American cities, could collect discarded American products for rock bottom prices and then ship them out. Once it has the products, the country could set up labor-intensive refurbishment centers. Through cannibalization and fabrication of key parts that wear out frequently these centers could bring these discarded products back to life. Some of the reconditioned cars and appliances would be sold in-country, but most would be sold in the international market at highly competitive prices.

Containerized Houses

It is not inconceivable that an entrepreneurial company in a third world country could start a house building company for export. Sections of houses would be built in a factory in, say, Brazil or Mexico, placed in containers and shipped to the construction site in the developed world, or elsewhere. House building materials are readily available, the necessary skills can be learned quickly, and the costs can be calculated accurately in advance.

Quality Hardware Manufacturing

Nor is it inconceivable that an aggressive company could start a quality hardware manufacturing facility for export specifically to the United States. Hardware presently sold in the United States is overpriced and often of poor quality, leaving the consumer virtually no alternative but to buy it or do without.

Quality Hand-Knotted Carpets

The development and expansion of quality, hand-knotted carpet industries in certain Middle Eastern and non-Middle Eastern countries might provide a profitable export business for an innovative MNC. Governments of countries not currently producing carpets might be especially interested in the high labor content, the high margins and foreign exchange returns, the advantages of having employees work in their homes. The technology is simple and inexpensive; the major investment would be training. Using strong marketing techniques, traditional markets could be expanded and new markets, such as those in the Middle East, opened.[25]

Advertising and Business-to-Business Promotion Services

Specializing in beginning or enlarging advertising and business-to-business marketing firms in third world countries allows an MNC not only to develop a strong worldwide service industry, but also to create a network it can call upon to move countertraded products.[26] For example, if an international advertising agency were to be established in an economically weak country (country A) and to send its consultants to other countries (countries B, C, and D) to help them with their marketing, foreign exchange in the form of fees would accrue to country A.

Insurance Industries

The market for insurance industries of all types is worldwide. General accident insurance in the Arab world has grown faster since World War II than anywhere else. In addition to the Arab countries, the countries of the Pacific Rim are prime candidates for insurance. MNC's major challenges include providing education on the benefits insurance provides and assuring host countries that they will help establish locally owned insurance companies.[27]

Most of the items listed above provide examples of how to start low-tech, labor-intensive businesses in developing countries. The last two items illustrate that services can likewise be exported across borders to generate foreign exchange.

USING BLOCKED FUNDS TO EXPAND AND INTERNATIONALIZE EDUCATION

How to Repatriate Blocked Funds

One of the major problems facing American corporations is freeing blocked funds. Blocked funds are created when the MNC exports a product into a socialist or third world country where it is sold for local currency, which—for one reason or another—cannot be converted back into hard currency. Because of financial instability and high inflation rates, under usual conditions blocked funds are used to purchase something produced locally in a type of countertrade transaction as is shown in Figure 6-2. Often real estate is purchased for want of anything else. But, because real estate cannot be removed, the MNC can be stuck with frozen assets for years.

Figure 6-2.

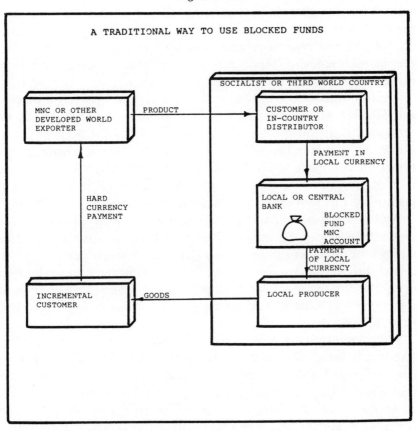

Today, American companies may have billions of dollars tied up in blocked funds around the world. How these funds are dispensed is a continuing source of worry among many international executives. Some of the methods used are secretive and not altogether legal. In general, the mechanisms for moving these funds are convoluted and inefficient.[28]

Back-to-back loans are sometimes used. In this procedure, Company A lends Company B a sum of hard currency outside the host country, and Company B lends Company A an equivalent sum of local currency inside the host country. Company B repatriates its earnings, and Company A uses the local currency for one of its projects. Usually Company A makes a nice profit for its service to Company B, getting more in soft currency than it gives in hard. In time, the loans are quietly forgotten by the companies. Host governments do not like this type of arrangement, as they believe they have lost the hard-currency expenditures that otherwise would have been made by Company A.[29]

Brokers who deal with blocked funds charge between 2 percent and 50 percent to convert them depending upon the political and economic situation of the country involved and the desperation of the MNC.[30] A number of managers have considered having movies filmed in countries where blocked funds exist, as a means of using the funds up. Pepsi used some of its blocked funds in a 50 percent investment in a film called *The Ninth Configuration.*[31]

Airline companies have found themselves with blocked funds around the world. Tickets are bought with local currency inside a number of third world countries, but the proceeds cannot be converted into hard currency because the governments are too short on cash. The International Air Transport Association (IATA) estimated that some $1.0 billion of its industry's money was tied up in blocked funds in 1983.[32]

Many companies put their blocked funds in short-term deposits. The World Bank uses buyback, investing its blocked funds in export companies and then selling them back to local entrepreneurs by taking and selling the exported products for hard currency.[33] Other companies take the creative countertrade route, investing blocked funds in exporting industries and selling the output for hard currency. Reynolds Aluminum, for example, decided to build a plant to make aluminum cans in Brazil for $52 million, in part because it had $11 million worth of blocked funds there.[34]

Creative countertrade is better able to repatriate funds blocked in the host country than is countertrade. Audley Shaw, the North American director of Jamaica National Investment Promotion, Ltd. (a government firm committed to helping MNCs invest in that country), will assist MNCs interested in investing blocked funds in Jamaican export businesses.

Mr. Shaw suggests that the MNC invest these funds in an exporting company within the host country and get the proceeds over time in hard-currency sales. By investing in export industries, he says, the company eventually can repatriate all of those funds.[35]

Figure 6-3.

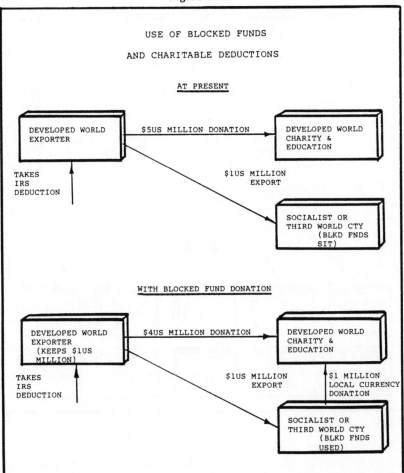

USE OF BLOCKED FUNDS

AND CHARITABLE DEDUCTIONS

AT PRESENT

DEVELOPED WORLD EXPORTER

$5US MILLION DONATION

DEVELOPED WORLD CHARITY & EDUCATION

TAKES IRS DEDUCTION

$1US MILLION EXPORT

SOCIALIST OR THIRD WORLD CTY (BLKD FNDS SIT)

WITH BLOCKED FUND DONATION

DEVELOPED WORLD EXPORTER (KEEPS $1US MILLION)

$4US MILLION DONATION

DEVELOPED WORLD CHARITY & EDUCATION

TAKES IRS DEDUCTION

$1US MILLION EXPORT

$1 MILLION LOCAL CURRENCY DONATION

SOCIALIST OR THIRD WORLD CTY (BLKD FNDS USED)

However, there is another alternative for freeing blocked funds: charitable deductions. Here, a U.S. exporter makes a $1 million sale inside a socialist or a third world country and also makes a standard annual $5 million donation to charity. As things stand at the end of the year, the corporation takes a $5 million charitable tax deduction, and has $1 million revenues on the books in blocked funds inside the host country.

In the lower part of Figure 6-3, the company does the exact same thing: It makes a $1 million sale into the host country, and it makes

Figure 6-4.

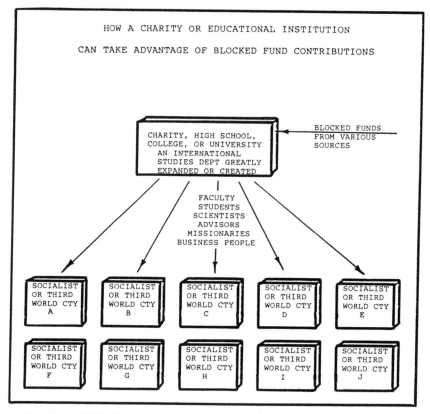

HOW A CHARITY OR EDUCATIONAL INSTITUTION

CAN TAKE ADVANTAGE OF BLOCKED FUND CONTRIBUTIONS

CHARITY, HIGH SCHOOL,
COLLEGE, OR UNIVERSITY
AN INTERNATIONAL
STUDIES DEPT GREATLY
EXPANDED OR CREATED

BLOCKED FUNDS
FROM VARIOUS
SOURCES

FACULTY
STUDENTS
SCIENTISTS
ADVISORS
MISSIONARIES
BUSINESS PEOPLE

SOCIALIST OR THIRD WORLD CTY A
SOCIALIST OR THIRD WORLD CTY B
SOCIALIST OR THIRD WORLD CTY C
SOCIALIST OR THIRD WORLD CTY D
SOCIALIST OR THIRD WORLD CTY E

SOCIALIST OR THIRD WORLD CTY F
SOCIALIST OR THIRD WORLD CTY G
SOCIALIST OR THIRD WORLD CTY H
SOCIALIST OR THIRD WORLD CTY I
SOCIALIST OR THIRD WORLD CTY J

its regular annual $5 million charitable contribution. Only this time it changes the currency mix. Instead of giving the full $5 million in hard currency to charity, the corporation gives $4 million in hard currency and transfers the equivalent of $1 million in local currency to the charity's account in the host country's central bank. The corporation then applies the $1 million worth of hard currency it otherwise would have donated, to revenues for products it sells inside the host country and takes the same charitable tax deduction.

A college or university could use the blocked funds to create or expand international programs. Figure 6-4 shows how a university can set up permanent branches in third world and socialist countries where it could send its students to study. The idea would be principally to educate the students about the local language, customs, history, government, economy and business environment, geography, and science. Blocked funds are often donated to educational institutions, but they can also be given to any American nonprofit organization that can make use of them overseas.[36]

Since companies have many requests for charitable contributions, why should they contribute to education in foreign countries? Is there a more compelling reason than just making use of blocked funds? Yes, there is. Americans need to be educated in foreign cultures. This can be best accomplished by studying and living overseas. Charitable contributions to foreign education would be designated particularly to support American students, not in American-only enclaves, but in foreign national universities.

Expanding Cultural and Business Horizons

A weakness of many Americans is their ignorance of foreign affairs and cultures. The world is growing more complex. The third world countries are developing economic, political, and military strength. Although the number of countries developing to newly industrialized status is growing linearly, the relationships among them and the rest of the world is growing geometrically. These new relationships engender new conditions, possibilities, and problems. Different technologies, economies, trade relationships, and political changes affect the increasing interactions among four basic players on the world business stage (Figure 6–5). Each has its own perspectives and goals of which the others must be aware. Those most sensitive to satisfying the others' needs will be the most successful in gaining their cooperation.

The result is shown in Figure 6–6. Within several years people with personal international experience in one or a number third world or socialist countries who participated in these programs would assume ever higher positions in business, government, and the nonprofit sectors of society. This would produce leaders who have a much better understanding of the world and an increased ability to make better informed decisions. Americans would be much more effective marketing their exports and could assume a far more enlightened role helping the world with its problems.

In the next illustration, we can see how the blocked funds would be transferred and some of the uses to which they would eventually

Figure 6-5.

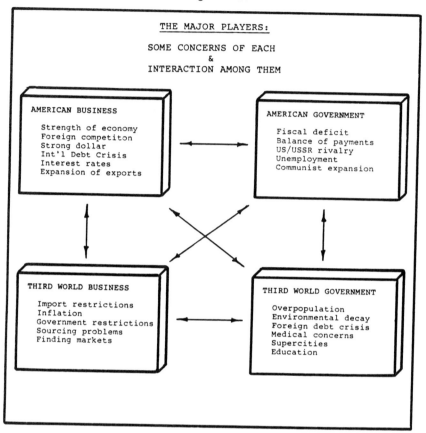

THE MAJOR PLAYERS:

SOME CONCERNS OF EACH
&
INTERACTION AMONG THEM

AMERICAN BUSINESS

Strength of economy
Foreign competiton
Strong dollar
Int'l Debt Crisis
Interest rates
Expansion of exports

AMERICAN GOVERNMENT

Fiscal deficit
Balance of payments
US/USSR rivalry
Unemployment
Communist expansion

THIRD WORLD BUSINESS

Import restrictions
Inflation
Government restrictions
Sourcing problems
Finding markets

THIRD WORLD GOVERNMENT

Overpopulation
Environmental decay
Foreign debt crisis
Medical concerns
Supercities
Education

be put. Faculty and students would come to study, bringing with them some hard currency of their own to supplement the blocked funds donations. Obviously, this would please the host country.

An entirely new industry would be created inside the host country through which it would sell its cultural, linguistic, historical, geographic, scientific, and cultural information to Americans (Figure 6-7). This would be a labor-intensive industry, consuming vast quantities of locally produced goods and services, increasing imports, and netting the host country increased foreign exchange in the process. No natural resources and few imports are needed to produce information, and it can be replicated many times at low expense, thus netting the country high margins.

Figure 6-6.

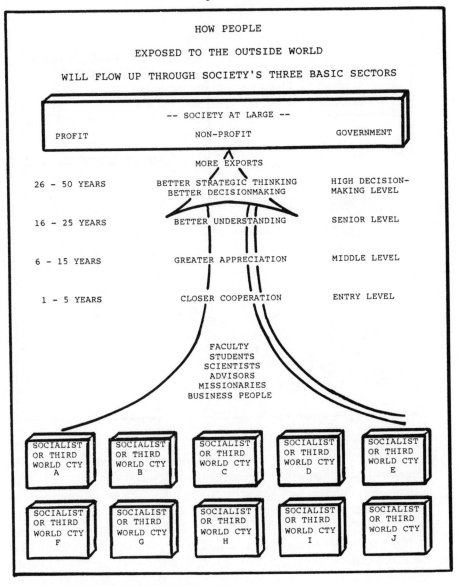

Figure 6–7.

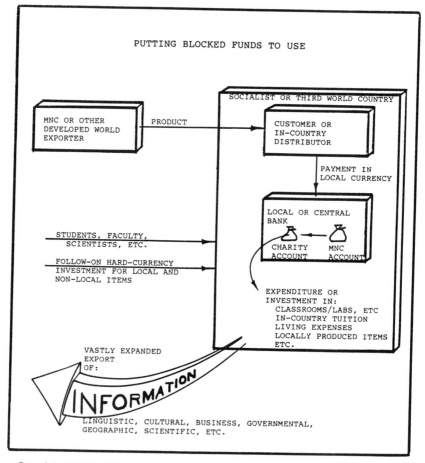

The long-range payoff is the development of human potential. As American and host country students meet and get to know each other, large numbers of the host country's youth will be exposed to educational, managerial, and technological transfer at the campus level.

Most third world countries should agree to this arrangement. The consumption of the blocked funds inside the host country expands employment and business and induces additional cash purchases. The high influx of foreign students and faculty causes a higher flow of ideas and technology into the host country. The greater exposure of outsiders to the culture will permit fairer news coverage in the developed world and increased investment due to lower perceived risk. But sweetest of all, there is no cannibalization of cash sales of its traditional exports.

American colleges operating in key third world countries can set up recruiting offices where they can offer their programs to potential students. Cooperative arrangements could be established allowing foreign students to study two years at the American college's campus in their own country—alongside the American students—and two more years on the U.S. home campus. In this manner, American education could be made available to a wider number of foreign students who otherwise might not be able to afford the full four year commitment to study and live inside the United States.

One of the major reasons for U.S. isolation is that the country is big, and all big countries have a tendency to be isolationist. For years the U.S. marketplace was large enough to absorb the growth potential for most American companies, which meant they did not have to sell abroad until they were strong and could devote teams of international specialists to the effort.

Additionally, the United States has only two close neighbors: Canada and Mexico. Canada has a society similar to that of the United States. The generally excellent relations between the United States and Canada have caused most Americans to take Canada for granted. Mexico, on the other hand, is situated far from Washington and until recently has figured little in the American mind. Despite this, U.S./Mexican and U.S./Canadian trade is extremely heavy.

U.S. cultural contact with other countries was minimal. More often than not, people came to the United States to do business rather than the other way around. While the country absorbed millions of immigrants, broad-based cultural ties with the old countries were usually lost after two generations.

Another reason for American isolationism is the narrow scope of the study of history in the American educational system. When much of the world was in a colonial status, the study of the history of Europe seemed enough, as these nations dominated most of the others and explained the roots of much of American thought. But once many former colonies become independent and began to assert themselves politically and economically, the gaps in an education focused solely on Western civilization became painfully obvious.

Presently, there are great voids in American historical understanding, which include the history of Arabs, Latin Americans, Africans,

Asia and Southeast Asia, the Soviet Union, and the Indian subcontinent. The absence of a colonial past has hurt the United States' ability to understand other cultures. In many respects Americans do not have as accurate a historical grasp of the Third World as do people from the colonial powers whose histories were intertwined with a number of these third world nations.

Even though, thanks to modern media, we know more about other cultures than ever before, there is more to learn. Contact with other countries has become so commonplace that international relations have taken on an increasingly personal tone. Similarly, with the American population bombarded daily with news of foreign events on television and in newspapers, people are demanding a greater say in the nation's international decisionmaking process.

On the whole, this trend is healthy and democratic. However, our understanding of foreign affairs has not kept pace with this increased level of awareness. Formerly, international relations was left to the province of diplomats, who spent their lives studying the intricacies of foreign cultures. But now, the decisions of these professionals are being overriden by a citizenry unschooled in the affairs of state and trade. Such a situation tends to produce reactive, shortsighted policies formulated by special interest groups, rather than policies that reflect the long-term interest of the nation as a whole.

Ironically, Americans have little idea how ignorant they are of the rest of the world. When they go overseas, they think they are coming in contact with a foreign culture, when, in fact, they are being catered to by a local industry of trained tourist professionals. Even scientists, scholars, and businesspersons when they travel abroad interact primarily with people who know our culture and speak English. Americans think they know foreign countries, when, in fact, they only know a thin veneer.[37]

Almost 20 percent of American manufacturing jobs rely on export, and some 33 percent of the profits of large American companies are made overseas.[38] Not surprisingly, their ignorance of other cultures frequently gets American business into trouble. For example, a number of years ago General Motors marketed the Nova in Brazil. But in Brazil Nova, or *no va*, means "does not work." Gerber Baby Foods shocked Filipino grocery shoppers when it introduced its products in that, putting a picture of a baby on the outside of the can. Gerber was unaware that it is the custom in that country to put a picture of the contents of the can on the label.[39]

Americans must inform themselves as much as possible about foreign affairs. At the end of the Second World War, the American economy constituted fully one half of the world economy. Today it is about one fourth. If the United States is to capitalize on today's opportunities, it is going to have to play a different game.

The Cost of International Ignorance.   The Foreign Corrupt Practices Act, a congressional blunder of the mid–1970s, has probably done more to lose U.S. exports than any other federal act. Intended as a political gesture to assuage the nation's feelings of guilt after Vietnam and Watergate, it was enacted with virtually no serious thought to its effect on U.S. business relations with other countries. This piece of legislation unilaterally tied the hands of American exporters to American standards of morality in a rough and tumble export world where in some cultures bribes and payoffs constitute acceptable ways of doing business. In other words, it put American business at a severe disadvantage.

In similar fashion, when the United States deregulated the U.S. telephone system it made no attempt to persuade other nations to deregulate theirs. As a result, foreign companies can bid for major contracts in the American system, whereas American telecommunications manufacturers are still locked out of bidding in many foreign countries.

The American grain embargo of the Soviet Union after Afghanistan was a futile gesture. Although it did give the Soviets pause, and caused them a certain amount of discomfort, it did not get them out of Afghanistan. It put the Soviets and many other nations as well on notice that the United States was not a reliable supplier and led the Soviets to extend their purchasing to Canada and Argentina. Today the U.S. farm system is close to financial ruin, to a certain extent because of those lost sales and the consequent introduction of new competitors.

The Tax Reform Act of 1978 was another blunder. Aware that many Americans resented their overseas compatriots getting any tax incentives and that American expatriates lacked significant political clout, Congress declared that Americans working in foreign countries had to pay full American income tax regardless of where they earned their money and what kind of taxes they paid in the countries where they lived. That provision was repealed the next year. But within that time, companies recalled to the United States a substantial percent of the American expatriate workforce. The American workforce was replaced by people of other nationalities, who promptly negotiated contracts and ordered supplies, not from American firms, but from companies in their own country.

In the early 1970s, President Nixon cancelled U.S. soybean exports because he was afraid of a shortage, and the domestic political repercussions that would ensue if the prices went too high. Japan, a large importer of soybeans, was incensed. The cutoff lasted only two weeks at which point the administration realized there was no shortage after all. Before the cutoff, Japan had received 80 percent of its soybean imports from the United States. But two weeks later the Japanese would accept no more than 20 percent of its soybean imports from the United States, having in that time diversified its purchases around the world.

The common thread running through these mistakes is American ignorance of an outside world. Additionally, they all cost the nation dearly. In each instance the situation would have been handled better if both public and government officials had had a better grasp of the international ramifications of their decisions.

Internationalizing College Curriculums.   There is a growing awareness in U.S. colleges and universities that their curricula must be internationalized. America badly needs experts in area studies, languages, and diplomacy in order to maintain its security and international standing. As the country becomes increasingly dependent upon global markets for its income,[40] foreign studies become of paramount importance. American academic institutions must overcome their parochial career interests, financial restraints, and lack of enthusiasm about the international world, and urge more of the nation's 9.5 million undergraduates to study abroad.[41]

Today, we are experiencing an almost geometric growth in our international interests and obligations. Despite that, language requirements in U.S. colleges and universities have actually declined in the last decade. While there are several thousand Japanese businessmen in New York city alone, most of whom are fluent in English, there are less than 100 American business people in Tokyo fluent in Japanese.[42] Americans studying abroad must rid themselves of the enclave mentality and live in homes of local residents instead of isolated villas. Similarly, they must attend schools in which classes are taught in the language of the country rather than in English.[43]

Blocked funds contributions would help business schools expand their international curriculums, give faculties exposure to different kinds of teaching, and create stronger personal international ties. Such activity would also increase college and university productivity because it would allow them to operate on a year-round basis. Additionally it would increase the number of paying students, and this without expanding facilities.

Some 350,000 foreign students study in the United States at over 2,500 colleges and universities. By contrast, the United States sends just over 30,500 of its 9.5 million undergraduates overseas, less than one third of one percent. This means that Iran, Taiwan and Venezuela—all third world nations, each with 27,000, 21,000 and 15,000 students in the U.S. respectively—have more than twice as many students in the United States as the United States has overseas! In addition, the total population of these nations (42 + 17 + 18 million respectively) is 77 million compared to some 234 million persons in the United States, which means that on a population basis the ratio is more like 6 to 1.[44]

Of foreign students studying in the United States, over 80 percent are funded from overseas, and over 90 percent eventually go back. Foreign students in the United States spend almost $2 billion on living expenses. Thus, the education of foreign students constitutes a hidden export industry in the United States, a growth industry with few strong competitors in the world marketplace.[45]

It has been documented that almost everyone who studies inside the United States leaves with a positive attitude toward America. They are supporters of the democratic capitalist system and tend to buy American products once they have gone back home. A very high portion of them assume influential positions in industry and government in their home countries.[46]

Sending college faculty to foreign countries to live and study would have a multipler affect because they, more than any other profession, communicate what they have learned to dozens and hundreds of others. Thus, a substantial number of U.S. teachers, well grounded in life outside the United States, would do much to encourage and prepare students to study abroad themselves.

Some large corporations could use blocked funds to finance their own educational seminars in third world countries and send their own executives there. Moreover, blocked funds could be donated to hospitals to send doctors around the world to administer to the needs of the poor and help train doctors in those countries. Other uses of blocked funds for donations include world tours for city symphony orchestras and international exhibitions of the collections of American art museums.

CREATIVE COUNTERTRADE SUCCESS FACTORS

Several success factors must be maintained in order for creative countertrade to work. The countertrade side must be both profitable and large enough to pull enough MNC products into the country. (If it is overly large the excess countertrade credits can conceivably be sold.) The MNC should control enough of the new business that the host nation cannot operate profitably without its participation. Otherwise it stands to get pushed out of the equation. For example, MNC control of the channels of distribution, the markets (MNC the chief customer), or a key element of the technology would suffice.

The MNC might wish to work at the grass roots level on both ends. Joint venture partners in both the developed and Third Worlds should be medium to small in size, thus making it difficult for them to walk away from the project without undue expense. Deals should be kept manageable. Work is done better in increments. Small entrepreneurs should be invited into the system.

The host government must agree to all essential points in the transaction in advance as in binding a contract. The evidence account should be in a bank or branch of the host country's central bank outside that country, thus making the earmarked foreign exchange generated by the creative countertrade operation more difficult to divert elsewhere. Capital expenditures and expenses should be kept as low as practicable at first until import restrictions are reduced and the MNC's product actually begins moving into the host country.

Managers will wish to avoid what happened to the Cummins Engine Company recently. In a countertrade deal, Cummins outfitted its headquarters in Ohio with $2 million worth of furniture made in Mexico in order to export an equivalent value of parts to its subsidiary there. After it had received and paid for the furniture, the Mexican government reneged on its promise to grant countertrade credits, and the subsidiary still does not have the parts.[47]

Ultimate MNC Goal

The idea of creative countertrade is to create not just one, but eventually a whole portfolio of small businesses in third world countries, exporting goods and services to the developed world (Figure 6–8).

Once a number of these businesses are created around the globe, the MNC will be better able to sell its products and repatriate its revenues in foreign countries. In addition, once the MNC has gained an expertise setting up small exporting companies inside third world countries, it can use this experience as a negotiating point when it sets up further business. If the MNC can combine present demand for its products with leverage gained from creative countertrade, sales to the third world countries can be increased substantially.

For best results, the creative countertrade operations should be strong enough to withstand a 30 percent drop in the dollar and keep running profitably,[48] and small enough so that the MNC does not take too great a loss should one fail.

For the MNC the ultimate goal is to have a number of small businesses in third world countries exporting to the industrialized world. This will allow the MNC to increase its international sales by maximizing its commercial leverage and lowering the landed cost of its products in foreign countries.

Ultimate Host Country Goal

Figure 6–9 illustrates the ultimate goal for the host country. As can be seen, numerous export businesses of all sizes and at all stages of development have been created with the help of MNCs.

Each start-up business employs people, teaches managerial and technical skills, earns foreign exchange, and gives the country more foreign exchange than that which was used to import the MNC's products. After a set period of time, the relationship between the MNC's product and the start-up company's exports might end, as it sometimes does in China. At this point the host country will have the full benefit of the entire net foreign exchange generated.

The country that helps create 100 viable businesses with 10 employees in each is better off, in the long run, than the one that helps create a large business staffed by 1000 people. The nation in which

Figure 6-8.

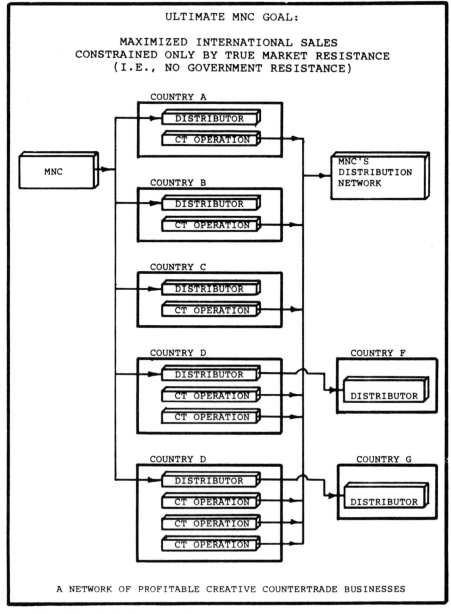

ULTIMATE MNC GOAL:

MAXIMIZED INTERNATIONAL SALES
CONSTRAINED ONLY BY TRUE MARKET RESISTANCE
(I.E., NO GOVERNMENT RESISTANCE)

COUNTRY A
DISTRIBUTOR
CT OPERATION

MNC

MNC'S
DISTRIBUTION
NETWORK

COUNTRY B
DISTRIBUTOR
CT OPERATION

COUNTRY C
DISTRIBUTOR
CT OPERATION

COUNTRY D
DISTRIBUTOR
CT OPERATION
CT OPERATION

COUNTRY F
DISTRIBUTOR

COUNTRY D
DISTRIBUTOR
CT OPERATION
CT OPERATION
CT OPERATION

COUNTRY G
DISTRIBUTOR

A NETWORK OF PROFITABLE CREATIVE COUNTERTRADE BUSINESSES

Figure 6-9.

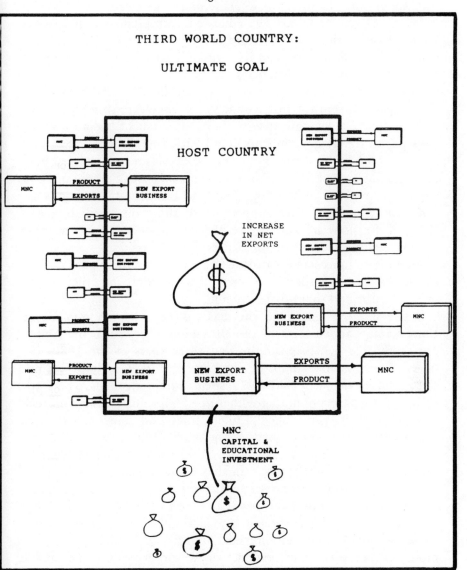

the small person is allowed to make high profits is the one that will prosper the most.

While nondeveloped nations should strive for high-tech transfer, they should not do so at the expense of less glamorous information transfer. All economies need an educated, entrepreneurial managerial human base to draw from before they can compete successfully in high tech. Anything less than this will only result in the trappings of high-tech without the substance.

The point to be stressed, however, is that the MNC and its business counterparts within the host country and elsewhere should be given the freedom by governments to chose the kinds of businesses they wish to set up. If governments stand back and allow private enterprise to work unhindered, net exports, employment, and revenues will grow at a faster rate. When governments stand back, an extra party is eliminated. With fewer people to consult vital decisions are made more quickly. The momentum of the project will be maintained if decisions are kept in the hands of those who have the most at stake and the greatest personal incentive to succeed.

Figure 6-10 gives an idea of differences in the investment climate of those countries that have succeeded in improving their GDPs over the years and those that have not.

Between 1970 and 1980 the small business community in the United States added most of the 20 million new jobs to the American workforce, whereas for the first three years of the 1980s the famed Fortune 500 companies collectively lost 3 million.[49] Since 1970, and particularly since 1979, small entrepreneurs have been the nation's driving economic growth force.[50] Ironically, the high tech industry with its gene splicing, fiber optics, and computers has created only a small portion of these new jobs.[51] It is the small entrepreneur, not the huge bank, MNC, or government who—left undisturbed—is any nation's most valuable resource. The greatest difference between those nations that succeed in the world marketplace and those that do not is the degree to which government and society give the entrepreneur free reign. The more these two groups presume to know about how entrepreneurs' businesses should be run, the more they wrap them in custom, policy, and procedure and hobble their chances of success. To accomplish their own objectives governments must take a non-interventionist role in the business sector, focusing their efforts on maintaining fair and orderly markets.

Figure 6-10.

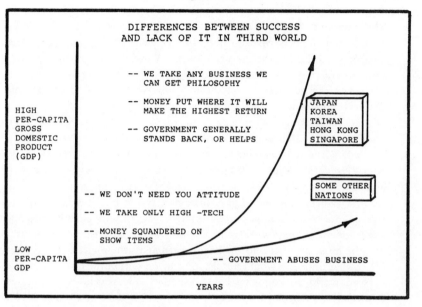

Those nations that equate the profit motive with greed or that are highly judgmental regarding the finer points between a little and excessive profit will not do well. Those nations that place emphasis on using the profit motive to improve their human capital in the low tech and managerial realm, where it can be most efficiently utilized will, in the long run, outpace those nations that do not. If there is success in the low tech/service sector, high-tech industries will follow. National patience is needed in this regard. Those countries that quietly put in place a strong managerial and skilled labor infrastructure will do the best in the long run.

Creative countertrade is specifically designed to maximize the prospects of both the MNC and the host country. If it succeeds as envisioned, it should help overcome the impasse between MNC overcapacity and lack of purchasing power in the Third World.

NOTES

1. Those nations that deliberately establish high quotas and tariffs or otherwise hinder imports with the intention of generating more countertrade overtures risk having the gesture backfire. What they may wind up with is no investment, no imports, and no business! Coercion rarely works, especially when those coerced have the additional options of doubling the market in country X when they get locked out of country Y.

2. Production Sharing International and Free Zone Authority Services, "Production Sharing Ventures: An Analysis," *Bobbin*, October 1984, p. 59.

3. Irving D. Canton, "Learning to Love the Service Economy," *Harvard Business Review* (May–June 1984): 89. In this article, Mr. Canton persuasively argues why manufacturers ought to consider service opportunities.

4. At first glance, third world governments may not like this aspect of creative countertrade. But just because MNCs have the opportunity to leave does not mean they will. Ironically, this aspect of creative countertrade may be most beneficial to the host governments themselves. It encourages MNCs that normally would not do so to invest within the host country.

   Third world governments could use the same psychology banks use. Banks allow their patrons the right to withdraw some or all their deposits from their savings and checking accounts at any time. This comforts depositors, who in turn put more money in the bank than otherwise would be the case.

5. Technoserve Inc., a seventeen-year-old nonprofit enterprise based in Norwalk, Connecticut, exports U.S. business know-how to third world countries. In 1983 it assisted 120 projects in 7 countries. Its success rate is reputed to be about 85 percent. Technoserve is one of a growing number of economic development consulting companies. *Business Week*, October 3, 1983, pp. 126, 130.

   If the MNC is able to establish consulting firms of this type in third world countries where it experiences governmental sales constraints, and properly package that expertise for the consumption of executives of other MNCs, it may be successful in bringing enough fees into the host country to gain it additional countertrade credits and other favorable treatment.

6. Certainly, the Chinese have the experience. Mainland China has sent more than $2.5 billion worth of aid to the rest of the Third World in the past three decades. In the four years from 1979 to 1982, China participated in 861 overseas construction contracts totalling $1.38 billion, according to Deborah A. Brautigam and Li Lu, "Doing Well by Doing Good: How Seven Chinese Firms Have Won Nearly $1.4 Billion in International Con-

struction Contracts," *China Business Review* (September/October 1983): 57, 58.

One may surmise that the vast amount of outside exposure gained through this activity has been the primary catalyst not only of the Chinese shifting their ideological direction so suddenly but also of their developing the managerial wherewithal to succeed. Yes, we all can learn from the Chinese.

7.   Allen R. Janger, "Organization of International Joint Ventures," *The Conference Board*, Report no. 787 (n.d.), p. 1.

8.   Ibid., p. 2. A fourth wanted to reduce political and financial risks, a fourth were induced by a need for raw materials, and a fifth entered joint ventures as a means of selling technology.

9.   Luis Alberto Monge, Financial Cooperation—Not Military: Private Enterprise and Government Working Together," *Vital Speeches*, January 15, 1984, p. 202. Costa Rica, which is steadfastly neutral and has no armed forced, is looking for financial cooperation from the United States, especially from the private sector.

10.   Stephen Kindel and Robert Teitelman, "If Only . . . ," *Forbes*, August 29, 1983, p. 126.

11.   *Business Week*, "A Shaken Caterpillar Retools to Take On a More Competitive World," November 5, 1984, p. 91.

12.   *Chemical Marketing Reporter*, "The U.S. Trade Deficit . . . ," September 26, 1983, p. 4.

13.   Janger, "Organization of International Joint Ventures."

14.   Barbara B. Cannon, "Joint Ventures: Hands the U.S. Company an Immediate Position in the Foreign Marketplace," *AIEM* (February 1982); 23.

15.   Peter Killing, "Technology Acquisition: License Agreement or Joint Venture," *Columbia Journal of World Business* (Fall 1980): 40.

16.   Peter Killing, "How to Make a Global Joint Venture Work," *Harvard Business Review* (May–June 1982): 120.

17.   Stephen E. Roulac, "Structuring the Joint Venture," *Mergers and Acquisitions* (Spring 1980): 4.

18.   Cannon, "Joint Ventures" is an excellent article on how to set up a joint venture.

19.   *Countertrade Outlook*, December 23, 1985, p. 5.

20.   This training would be especially valuable for those wishing eventually to start their own businesses.

21.   William A. Delphos, *Washington's Best Kept Secrets: A U.S. Government Guide to International Business* (New York: John Wiley & Sons, 1984), pp. 7, 166.

22.   Ibid., p. 159.

23.   *Countertrade Outlook*, January 7, 1985, p. 2; November 5, 1984, p. 1.

24. Ruth Anne Davis, chair of the American Society of Interior Designers, thought the idea had possibilities. Meeting with author, Washington, D.C., December 1984.

25. "Hand-knotted Carpets—Market Openings for Quality Goods," *International Trade Forum*, July/September 1984, pp. 12–17.

26. Julia Michaels, "Industrial Marketing a Scarce Commodity: Brazilian Ad Structure Hampers Expansion," *Advertising Age*, October 10, 1985, p. 34.

27. Basim A. Faris, "The Influence of the New-Found Wealth on Insurance in the Arab World," *International Business Monitor*, June/July/August 1984, pp. 4–8; "First Life Insurance Trade Mission Breaks New Ground in Far East," *Business America*, May 27, 1985, pp. 22–23.

28. John C. Perham, "The Mysterious Market in Blocked Accounts," *Duns Review*, October 1976, pp. 93–94.

29. Ibid.

30. Ibid.

31. *Countertrade Outlook*, October 21, 1985, p. 3.

32. "Cash the Airlines Can't Use," *Business Week*, April 19, 1983, p. 96J.

33. *Countertrade Outlook*, February 13, 1984, p. 1.

34. *Countertrade Outlook*, December 9, 1985, p. 6.

35. The explicit purpose of this organization is to make investment in Jamaica as easy as possible for the MNC. Mr. Shaw is quite an entrepreneur himself and will help in any way possible.

36. Blocked funds have been used to finance Fulbright Scholarships. See James M. Barkas, "Offsets as an Instrument of Yugoslav Economic Development, Part I," *Countertrade and Barter Quarterly* (Spring 1986): 13.

37. Michael Howard, "The Bewildered American RAJ: Reflections on a Democracy's Foreign Policy," *Harpers*, March 1985, pp. 55–60.

38. Charles W. Bray, III, "Parochial America," *Christian Science Monitor*, March 24, 1981, p. 23.

39. Howard LaFranchi, "Bringing a Global Perspective to the Ivory Tower," *Christian Science Monitor*, May 14, 1985, p. 19.

40. Ibid.

41. Howard LaFranchi, "Overseas Study—An Underused Option for U.S. Students," *Christian Science Monitor*, May 15, 1984, p. 23.

42. Bray, "Parochial America."

43. LcFranchi, "Bringing a Global Perspective to the Ivory Tower."

44. Howard LaFranchi, "American Schooling: A Sought-After 'Export'," *Christian Science Monitor*, May 17, 1984, p. 23.

45. Howard LaFranchi, "Foreign Students at U.S. Colleges: The Benefits Are Mutual," *Christian Science Monitor*, May 18, 1984, p. 24.

46. Ibid.

47. *Countertrade Outlook*, February 27, 1984, p. 1; October 29, 1984, p. 2.

48. How much of an impact a shift in the value of the dollar would have depends upon the percentage of the costs of the countertraded goods tied to the dollar that would not figure in the equation. Goods that have a high value added content outside the host country may be more resistant to price and dollar shifts than products where the value added content is primarily domestic.

49. Thomas R. Horton, "Entrepreneurialism Lives!" *Credit and Financial Management* 86, no. 9 (October 1984): 29–30; James L. Freelay, "The Service Economy: An Entrepreneurial Era," *Review of Business* 7, no. 1 (Summer 1985): 17–18.

50. Joseph Duncan, "The Job Market Looks Up," *Duns Business Month*, April 1983, pp. 60–61.

51. Courtenay Slater, "Getting High on Technology," *American Demographics*, November 1983, pp. 40–41.

7 THE FUTURE OF COUNTERTRADE

What will determine countertrade's future is the balance between (1) the benefit it gives countertrading parties, and (2) the negative effects of countertrade on world and national economies as perceived by powerful interests such as developed world governments and international organizations.

Countertrade raises an old question but in the context of the world economy: when do people working for their own profit begin hurting the group as a whole? Not only is there no easy answer to this question, most likely there will never be an answer upon which everyone can agree. Ideology plays a part: invisible hand versus anti-trust style regulation, or viewed from another angle, protectionism versus free trade. The fact that it is next to impossible to measure individual gains versus harm to the group—much less to balance them—means that the answer will always be subjective and there-fore political. As with most political problems, the outcome lies with who's ox is being gored and what can be done about it.

Figure 7-1 charts different directions predicted for countertrade. As one might expect, those who like it are more optimistic about its future than those who do not. Our research suggests that it is unlikely countertrade will average much beyond the 10 to 15 percent level of total world trade. The use of it on the international scene will oscillate rather than experience a steady rise. As world economic conditions shift, so will countertrade.

Figure 7-1.

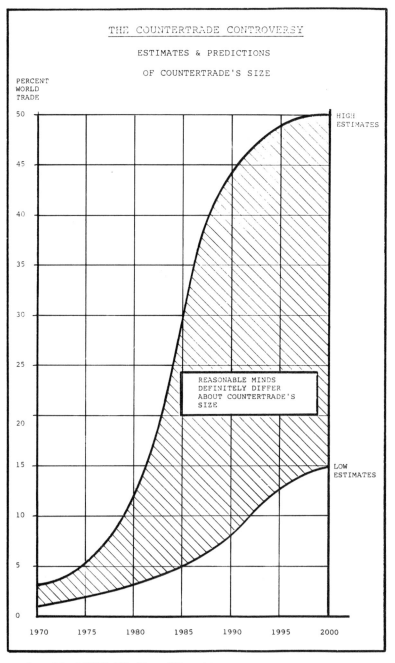

Figure 7-2.

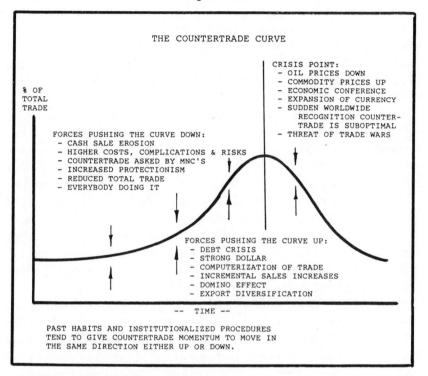

THE COUNTERTRADE CURVE

CRISIS POINT:
- OIL PRICES DOWN
- COMMODITY PRICES UP
- ECONOMIC CONFERENCE
- EXPANSION OF CURRENCY
- SUDDEN WORLDWIDE
  RECOGNITION COUNTER-
  TRADE IS SUBOPTIMAL
- THREAT OF TRADE WARS

% OF
TOTAL
TRADE

FORCES PUSHING THE CURVE DOWN:
- CASH SALE EROSION
- HIGHER COSTS, COMPLICATIONS & RISKS
- COUNTERTRADE ASKED BY MNC'S
- INCREASED PROTECTIONISM
- REDUCED TOTAL TRADE
- EVERYBODY DOING IT

FORCES PUSHING THE CURVE UP:
- DEBT CRISIS
- STRONG DOLLAR
- COMPUTERIZATION OF TRADE
- INCREMENTAL SALES INCREASES
- DOMINO EFFECT
- EXPORT DIVERSIFICATION

-- TIME --

PAST HABITS AND INSTITUTIONALIZED PROCEDURES
TEND TO GIVE COUNTERTRADE MOMENTUM TO MOVE IN
THE SAME DIRECTION EITHER UP OR DOWN.

As Figure 7-2 shows, a number of factors influence the use of traditional countertrade. In the next several years, the volume of countertrade may well rise, then suffer a sudden decline, and in a number of years again make a comeback.

By nature, countertrade can be expected to fluctuate as a percent of world trade. To some extent its cyclical nature resembles that of the U.S. trading stamp industry. In 1896, when S&H first established Green Stamp gift redemption centers, the business took off. Trading stamp activity rose until World War I but then declined until 1951. The latest rising trend began in 1951 and ended just after the 1973 oil embargo.[1]

As with international trade, the grocery and gas station businesses are extremely competitive because the customer has so many stores and stations from which to choose. Objections to trading stamps are similar to those leveled against countertrade: added costs, availability of promotional alternatives, no added quality, universal availability, and the practice of forcing people to pay for things they do not necessarily want.

Thus, trading stamps were introduced, grew rapidly, declined, and later rose, starting the cycle once again. Countertrade, while always providing a key mechanism for expanding trade at the margin and creating opportunities where none were visible before, will experience similar cyclical fluctuations.

Some kind of enforcement mechanism, the result perhaps of a high-level, multinational economic conference, would cause a decline in countertrade. Sanctions against countertrading countries could come in the form of disciplinary measures such as increased trade barriers preventing sales of countertraded goods or the withholding of foreign aid and/or international loans. But given the weakened state of many debtor nations and the consequent loan exposure of the developed world countries, it is unlikely that any sanctions imposed will be severe. The growth of countertrade may stop and fall to lower levels of its own accord, thus eliminating the need for developed world governments to act to limit it.

On the other hand, if developed world governments do not intervene, what set of events will cause the use of countertrade to drop by itself? As the debt crisis is countertrade's raison d'etre, one way of ending it would be a huge increase of world liquidity through the expansion of one or several of the world's major currencies such as the dollar, the yen, the pound, the Deutschmark, or SDRs. Economists believe this probably will not happen, however, and cite the indebted state of developed world governments, the precarious position of large banks and the inflationary effect such a currency expansion would have on the developed world economies.[2]

Change may already have begun. The reduction of oil prices in early 1986 could shift as much as $130 billion in payments annually from oil producers to oil consumers. Since most (but not all) oil consumers are countries with large debts, this oil transfer will free needed cash. Moreover, if oil prices remain low for several years, the world economy may come to life, thus driving up commodity prices and giving debtor nations even more foreign exchange.

Rapid economic growth may reduce pressures to capitalize on every available trading opportunity, thus forcing a decline in the relative importance of countertrade. A recession or slow growth would, on the other hand, increase the incentives among all parties to grab for themselves trade opportunities by demanding countertrade.

A second factor concerns political relations among the West and the Soviet Union and its allies. If, for political reasons, trade is restricted or eliminated, a possible arena for countertrade will have been eliminated. Conversely, a political decision by the West to expand trade with these nonmarket economics would accelerate the use of countertrade. Because East–West relations and the total level of world economic growth directly affect the use of countertrade, the amount of countertrade done as a percentage of world trade would thus be cyclical rather than steady.

Countries in the Third World see countertrade as a way out of some of their economic problems. They believe that under the right circumstances, countertrade can be a positive force in international trade. They believe it has the following advantages:

1. Keeps essential imports open
2. Conserves foreign exchange
3. Helps maintain exports
4. Increases South–South trade
5. Balances accounts between certain countries that have gotten too far out of balance
6. Encourages import substitution.[3]

Opinions between the Developed and Third Worlds are divided. Many in third world nations believe that if countertrade works on a deal-by-deal basis—where no suitable alternatives are available—it should be done. They believe that countertrade is helping South–South trade. On the other hand, many in the developed world believe that in order to maintain the integrity of the free trade system countertrade should be avoided altogether.

Countertrade may still be so new that many countries have not thought through its ramifications. In spite of its apparent advantages, it may prove to work against third world countries in the long-run. By and large, third world countries do not have the negotiating leverage of their trading partners in the developed world. The drawbacks discussed may simply convince major countertrade participants that countertrade has a limited place in international trade.

The international community may first have to experience the disadvantages of countertrade before it fully appreciates the benefits of traditional ways of doing business. Because it is so new, the long-term impact of countertrade is yet to be determined. The ultimate conclusion of the international community may be that while countertrade is convenient, nothing comes for free.

Already, countertrade has not met the expectations of some third world countries. Indonesia, one of countertrade's principal proponents, no longer mandates countertrade because that nation was losing cash sales. The Countertrade Market Share Wheel, discussed in Chapter 4 (Figure 4-1), showed how competitor nations can cannibalize each other's sales through countertrade. The Indonesians discovered something worse: they had no way to monitor the whereabouts of their world exports once they left the country. To their chagrin, their exports wound up with end users who were regular cash purchasers. Malaysia, too, has taken its commodities off the countertrade list. Since commodities are the bulk of its exports, Malaysia countertrades less than before.[4]

China may be doing less countertrade than meets the eye. It is true that China has completed many deals in the past decade. But on closer look, the vast majority of them are small cottage industry transactions taking place between China and Hong Kong. Countertrade with MNCs is not as easy or commonplace as supposed due to Chinese lack of organization and the fact that the Chinese try to drive too hard a bargain. In any event, the Chinese make certain the MNC pays the full cost of doing countertrade.[5]

In the long run, excluding the Socialist bloc, countertrade's natural upper limit may be confined to incremental exports, lame trade that cannot be moved by itself and military offsets. As Figure 7-3 suggests, last year's incremental (i.e. new) exports are this year's traditional sales. Suppose in the figure, country Z in year one uses countertrade to create incremental exports. In year two it uses its first year's countertrade deal to hold onto year one's incremental exports, and uses more countertrade to get year two's incremental exports. Eventually, the exports gained by countertrade several years earlier will revert to cash sales. The figure shows year one's worth of incremental exports—received and maintained up to that time by countertrade—being shifted to cash sales.

This suggests that countertrade is inherently self-limiting as a percent of world trade. Certainly it will grow, but so too will total world trade. All countries want incremental exports, and many will use countertrade to get them. But most countries want to discard the countertrade mechanism as soon as possible after establishing or expanding the new export industries in order to get the cash. The

Figure 7-3.

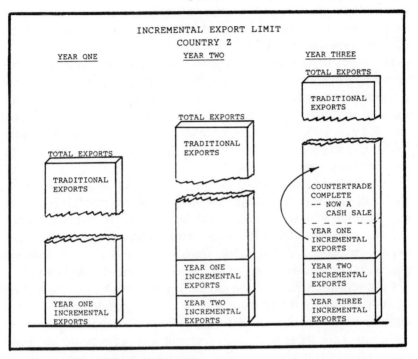

Copyright © 1987, Elderkin and Norquist.

amount of time it takes for this to happen varies from one transaction to the next. Creative countertrade and some buybacks can extend over fifteen years or more. But most countertrade deals come to an end sometime, and for those countries that have established high-cash- potential export markets, the sooner it ends the better.

Military offsets will remain a major element of countertrade for years to come. But even there one finds growing resistance due to the increased competitiveness in the arms manufacturing industry. Because of this the growth of offsets may level off. Besides the production from Western Europe and the Eastern Bloc countries, nations such as Brazil, Israel, South Korea, and China now make arms for export, and their technology is improving. Military offsets from the United States have been a major factor in aiding nonsocialist countries effectively to replicate the U.S. arms industry.

There is a growing concern in the United States Government that it can no longer afford to be lackadaisical about diplomatic and military secrets. If it discovers that the nation is losing its technological and military edge by giving away too much through offsets, it may clamp down on companies doing offsets regardless of their short-term loss of sales. So the future of military offsets—at least from the American standpoint—is by no means assured.

Debate as to whether countertrade is by nature temporary or permanent misses the point. Countertrade will be a permanent fixture in the world marketplace, although a smaller one than many would suppose. Countertrade helps stabilize an economic situation unbalanced by a lack of foreign exchange, uncertainty on fluctuating exchange rates and commodity prices, and efforts to restructure the industrial capacity of the South.

Countertrade will be used as long as it works. Business people are above all practical. Despite the weaknesses of free trade, it is unlikely countertrade will grow unimpeded because of its own weaknesses. On the other hand, within those areas where it works the best—export increase, righting trade imbalances, and moving distressed goods—countertrade is a superb trade vehicle and should be used.

Countertrade's place in economic history will be determined not by its size but by its ultimate benefit to world trade. In all its forms countertrade's catalytic effect on third world economic growth will far outdistance its growth in size. It will light a fire under the newly developing export sectors of host countries and get them growing at much faster rates. Because the growth of the third world export sector—along with the corresponding growth of its import sector—will continue to be a pressing economic problem, creative countertrade should be allowed to help achieve this important end.

We have seen that countertrade, and especially creative countertrade, is a good vehicle for helping cash-poor countries because it finds ways for private interests to make a profit by helping these countries. By so doing it uses the entrepreneurial spirit, the strongest tool of democratic capitalism, to augment government aid and commercial lending.

Were countertrade of this sort promoted by the major governments and interests of the developed world, rather than denigrated by them, the progress of economic and social reform in countries where communism is a danger would be greatly enhanced. Not only might billions of tax dollars be saved by avoiding future bailouts after certain countries had defaulted on their loans, the world would be a safer place for the West.

Even in the strictest context of protectionism, it is difficult to brand as "bad" a system that expands a country's exports rather than its imports, as countertrade clearly does. But within the context of using countertrade to help solve the problems of the Third World vis-à-vis the East–West struggle, countertrade may be the bargain of the century.

NOTES

1. John C. Griffin, Jr., and William Rouse, "Countertrade as a Third World Strategy of Development," *Third World Quarterly* (January 1986): 177–204.
2. Ed Zotti, "They Take a Licking, But Keep on Sticking," *Advertising Age*, March 15, pp. M34–35.
3. *Countertrade Outlook*, January 7, 1986, p. 1.
4. Wayne Forrest, "Countertrade in the Pacific Basin Nations," The Countertrade Roundtable of New York, June 5, 1986.
5. Gabriel Zalka, "Countertrade in the Pacific Basin Nations," The Countertrade Roundtable of New York, June 5, 1986.

APPENDIXES

APPENDIX A

THE OFFSET FORMULA

Many MNCs are in a weak bargaining position until they can show the host government that it will not lose foreign exchange on the transaction. Some consumer product MNCs actually have their products banned in third world countries. But if they can demonstrate that hard currency will not be lost on the deal, the host government generally will be much more agreeable.

For example, suppose the MNC wishes to sell $1,000,000 worth of its product into the host country, but cannot because of quotas and tariffs. In response to this, suppose the MNC decides to set up a data entry service in the host country in a creative countertrade operation. What minimum revenues does the data entry service have to earn in order to get in all the MNC's product and not drain any of the country's foreign exchange?

As discussed, the value of the countertraded goods can be broken into a value added, inside the country component and a foreign content component. Therefore, in order for there to be no foreign exchange drain, the value of the MNC's product must equal the domestic value added content of the countertraded goods.

In this manner, the host country loses no foreign exchange, because the offset is over 100 percent and is now covering the foreign exchange expended to produce the countertraded goods. Under these conditions the host government should be persuaded to eliminate all import restrictions on the MNC's products coming into the country.

Therefore, the MNC would be giving the host country its product plus some cash in exchange for the countertraded goods.

Continuing this example, let's say there is a 70 percent domestic value added content, comprised primarily of labor, for data entry services. Assume the rest—equipment, overhead, out-of-country supervision, etc.—is the foreign content component.

In terms of a formula, the transaction would look like this:

Let P = Value of the products it wishes to sell the host country

C = Cash

VAO = Value of the countertraded goods added outside the host country (i.e., imports required to produce them)

VAI = Value of the countertraded goods added inside the host country (i.e., the domestic content)

Then when the host government loses no foreign exchange:

P = VAI

C = VAO

and

P + C = VAO + VAI

Thus, the MNC's product plus cash equals the domestic value added plus the foreign content of the countertraded goods. This, in turn, equals the total value of what the MNC gives up.

In our example, the value of the MNC's product equals the domestic value added component of the countertraded services. In other words, $100,000 equals 70 percent of the services. Thus, solving the problem through simultaneous equations, the total value of the creative countertrade operation would be $143,000 (essentially, $100,000 divided by 70 percent.) This puts the offset at 143 percent, for a zero exchange drain. The important thing to note, however, is that if the countertrade side is either profitable or a breakeven proposition, larger offsets can be allowed thus getting more product into the country.

JAMAICA AND CREATIVE COUNTERTRADE

Jamaica has a small market for MNC products. With a population of only 2.2 million persons to begin with, it is poor by developed world standards and a small purchaser of MNC consumer products.

However, Jamaica has several interesting aspects. It is English speaking and thinks along Western lines, thus making it an easy third world business laboratory for American MNCs. Jamaica has a highly business-oriented government, willing to experiment, brilliantly led, and administrated by highly competent government officials. The Jamaican Government has a close relationship with the Reagan Administration, itself strongly pro–business. Thus, solid business contacts can be made fairly easily in both governments.

If the Jamaican government, or one like it, could be persuaded to pass the selective tariff reduction concept into law and use this legislation effectively, it would generate a significant interest in the United States. If such a plan worked as envisioned, other governments might well be persuaded to follow suit.

Experimentation is the best approach for governments to take in the beginning. Once the host country has several MNCs start up small entrepreneurial firms in its country, it can discover the best formula and instruct other MNCs to take the same approach. These procedures can then be packaged and traded to MNCs in seminar and book form in exchange for an agreement from those corporations to make a best-effort approach to starting up new businesses there.

INDEX

213

Barclays Bank, 69
Barter, 1-2, 6, 9, 31, 43, 79
BATIS International, 26
Bauxite, 5, 50, 63, 112
Belgium, 103
Belize, 117
Bilateral clearing account, 10, 37, 51;
    political risks, 90-91
Bilateral trade, 103-105, 116
Blocked funds, xv; and cultural
    exchange programs, 177-183; and
    education programs, 175-177,
    185-186; repatriation, 172-175
Blue-collar employment, 111, 113
Boeing Aircraft, 3, 5, 126-127
Boles World Trade Corp., 78
Bolivia, 51
Bombardier of Canada, 103
Boylan, Mr., 84
Brazil, xiv, 41, 51, 116, 156, 159;
    agricultural trade, 7, 165-166;
    aluminum cans, 174; arms sales, 203;
    automobiles, 114, 182; capital flight,
    142; Commission for the Concession
    of Fiscal Benefits to Special Export
    Programs, 147; import licenses, 13;
    and oil, 35; trading companies, 78;
    and United States, 64; and Xerox,
    166
Breach of contract insurance, 85
Bretton Woods, 104
Bulgaria, 44
Burma, 103-104
Buybacks, 3-4, 9, 51, 101-103, 112,
    121; and China, 3, 112, 119, 169;
    and Eastern Europe, 3, 44, 101, 119;
    and Israel, 48; percent of trade, 6

C. Itoh and Company, Ltd., 76
Cameron Petroleum, Inc., 55
Camp David Accord, 64
Canada, 152 n. 2, 181, 183; arms
    purchases, 102-103; countertrade,
    8, 46, 103
Cannon, Barbara, 160
Cannon Consulting, 160
Capital flight, 142
Capital transfer and trade, 111,
    113-114; and countertrade,
    135-136, 141-142
Cardin, Pierre, 128
Carem-Andruet, Hector, 72

Caribbean, 49-51, 108-109, 117;
    investment decision grid, 156; and
    MNCs, 118; production sharing, 165
Caribbean Basin Initiative, 117,
    164-165
Caribbean Basin Investment Exposi-
    tion, 108
Carpets, 171
Cash sales, countertrade effects on, xv,
    89-92, 151
Castro, Fidel, 85, 118
Caterpillar Tractor Company, 159
CBS, 3
Central America, 50-51
Central Bank of Vienna, 69
Central banks, 13, 20, 27, 73
Certifications, 67-69
Charitable donations, 175-177
Chase Manhattan, 69, 71-72
Chemical Bank, 69
Chemical industry, xiii, 56, 159
Cheney Group, 107
Chile, 51-52
China, 32, 128-129, 131; agricultural
    trade, 2; arms sales, 203; buybacks,
    3, 112, 119, 169; and creative
    countertrade, 156, 157, 187, 202;
    credit rating, 135-136; foreign aid
    programs, 117, 192-193 n. 6; and
    Hong Kong, 3, 90, 169, 202; and
    international trade credits, 75; and
    Japan, 2; and MNCs, 118; reciproc-
    ity, 10; Red Guard, 115, 117; satel-
    lites, 114; skiing, 167; television, 3;
    turnkey facilities; volume of counter-
    trade, 41
Chori Co., Ltd., 76
Chromite, 63
Chrysler, 5, 55, 56
Chubb, 83
CIGNA World Wide, 84
Citibank, 69, 70
Cobalt, 63
Coca-Cola, 5, 55, 122
Coffee beans, 61
Colombia, 11, 51, 156
Clearing account. See Bilateral clearing
    account
Commodities, xiii, 60-61, 90; and
    buybacks, 101; demand, 34; dis-
    counts, 39, 60; exchanges, 20; and
    industrial economies, 111, 112;

ABOUT THE AUTHORS

Kenton W. Elderkin is the president of Elderkin & Associates, a management consulting practice engaged in countertrade seminars and business, business research, and business writing. He is also president of the Countertrade Forum of New England. After having served twice in Vietnam, he joined the Polaroid Corporation, where he wrote numerous reports and studies as countertrade manager. He holds a B.S. in Naval Science and Foreign Affairs from the U.S. Naval Academy, a Certificate de Lettres from the Sorbonne in Paris, France, a J.D. from Florida State University, and an MBA in finance from Northeastern University.

Warren E. Norquist is director of worldwide purchasing for the Polaroid Corporation and is responsible for all purchases of materials and services by Polaroid, both domestic and international. He was previously responsible for Worldwide Quality and Reliability. An American Society for Quality Control fellow, Norquist was also on that society's board for ten years. He is a former president of the Engineering Societies of New England and was on the board of the American national Standards Institute. He is now chairman of the Certification Policy Board of the National Association of Purchasing Management. He is the creator of Zero Base Pricing™. Norquist received a B.S. degree in engineering from the University of Michigan and an MBA with Distinction from the Harvard Business School.